A
Treasury of Story Sermons
for Children

A
Treasury of Story Sermons
for Children

Edited by

CHARLES L. WALLIS

BAKER BOOK HOUSE
Grand Rapids, Michigan

First printing, January 1975
Second printing, March 1976
Third printing, November 1979
Fourth printing, February 1982

© 1957 by Charles L. Wallis
Reprinted 1975 by Baker Book House Company
with the permission of
Harper & Row, Publishers, Incorporated
Library of Congress Catalog Card Number: 57-7343
ISBN: 0-8010-9556-5
Printed in the United States of America

Special acknowledgment is made to the following who have granted permission for the reprinting of copyrighted material from the books listed below:

ABINGDON PRESS for "God's Scales" from *Story Sermons and Plans for the Junior Church* by Marian Walter Gannaway, copyright 1949 by Pierce & Smith; "Three Boys and a Dog" from *Stories for Junior Worship* by Alice Geer Kelsey, copyright 1941 by Whitmore & Stone; "The Herald of the Great King" from *More Stories for Junior Worship* by Alice Geer Kelsey, copyright 1948 by Stone & Pierce; "Snowflakes" from *The Teakwood Pulpit and Other Stories for Junior Worship* by Alice Geer Kelsey, copyright 1950 by Pierce & Smith.

THE CAREY KINGSGATE PRESS, LTD. for "A Preacher with Four Eyes" from *Now, Children!* by J. R. Edwards.

JAMES CLARKE & CO., LTD., for "The Little That Is Much" from *Good Measure* by J. Rodger Lyle.

THE EPWORTH PRESS for "The Boy with Many Friends" from *Traffic Lights* by R. E. Thomas; "Making Music" from *Listen, Children!* by Rita F. Snowden; extract from "Solid Sunshine" from *Solid Sunshine* by H. Lovering Picken; "What's in a Balloon?" from *Truth—to Tell* by H. Lovering Picken; extract from "The Order of Near Enough" from *Wits End Corner* by T. Greener Gardner.

HARPER & BROTHERS for "A Man Who Never Became Angry" and "The Unknown Scout" from *Story Sermons from Literature and Art* by Walter Dudley Cavert, copyright 1939 by Harper & Brothers; "The Clock without Hands" from *New Story Talks to Boys and Girls* by Howard J. Chidley, copyright 1929 by Harper & Brothers; "Do You Own Your Face?" from *The Junior Church in Action*, copyright 1921 by Harper & Brothers; "The Open Door" from *75 Stories for the Worship Hour* by Margaret W. Eggleston, copyright 1929 by Harper & Brothers; "I Would Be True" from *The Use of the Story in Religious Education* by Margaret W. Eggleston, copyright 1936 by Harper & Brothers; "I Know a Path" from *40 Stories for the Church, School and Home* by Margaret W. Eggleston, copyright 1939 by Harper & Brothers; "Growing toward God" from *30 Stories I Like to Tell* by Margaret W. Eggleston, copyright 1949 by Harper & Brothers; "The Magic Violin," "The Second Violin" and "Who Owns the Lighthouse?" from *Stewardship Stories* by Guy L. Morrill, copyright 1941 by Harper & Brothers;

To
Quentin T. Lightner
Pastor, Teacher, and Confidant
of Youth

CONTENTS

Contents

Contents

Contents

Contents

PREFACE

"Let the children come to me, and do not hinder them; for to such belongs the kingdom of heaven" (Matt. 19:14, RSV). Christ's invitation to children has always been made vivid and personal through the use of stories. The world of children and the spiritual world meet when the storyteller quickens the imagination through narratives that have plenty of action, personality, and dialogue so that their religious truth somehow carries a sense of immediacy.

The materials in this book combine the tradition of the storyteller's craft and the homiletic heritage of the pulpit. For instructional purposes the story-sermon enhances the vitality of narration with the textual and thematic exposition of the sermon.

In this anthology the one hundred and fourteen story-sermons represent the varied emphases of Christian education. The collection is designed for use in church worship, children's church, church school assemblies and classes, and in the home. Each story-sermon has a distinctive spiritual message which, without being too pointedly didactic, mirrors the many interests of children, their love of adventure, their fascination for biblical and national heroes, and their natural curiosity about the worlds of nature and people. More than one-third of the story-sermons were written expressly for this volume. At the back of the book is a topical index, an index of texts, and an index according to the special days and seasons of the church year. Because most of the materials can be readily adapted as occasion may require, the story-sermons have not been graded. An asterisk (*) at the end of a story-sermon indicates that it has been slightly adapted or abbreviated.

The story-sermon is a natural vehicle for the instruction of children. "Any educational approach which presumes to relate itself to life," Hulda Niebuhr has written, "will use the story, for the story has its roots in life, it is life condensed, life in spotlight, it is of the essence of life itself." Long ago Jesus showed how the minds of children, and of adults too, can through stories be awakened to new experiences, new appreciations, and new truths. Occasionally, however, a specialist in children's literature objects to stories which are written specifically to teach a lesson. Such a suggestion, if taken without discrimination, would lead to an elimination from the vast library of juvenile fiction much that is superior.

If a storyteller's purpose is merely to amuse or to heighten the child's imaginative faculty, then the "moral" is superfluous. But if stories are to become channels through which a child may develop sound habits, learn lessons, or broaden his spiritual experiences, then a tale with a moral is a commendable tool in character-training. The parables of Jesus were never ends in themselves. Their implications embraced the fullest life experience and they were, of course, unashamedly moral. The objection to moralizing in storytelling is probably a result of the way in which some writers tack morals onto their yarns. The "lesson" best makes its point when it is implicit in the story. If the purpose of the story is clear to the storyteller, the children will easily surmise its meaning and may have fun catching on.

Dorothy Canfield Fisher offers a pointed comment:

> Why do up-to-date, sophisticated or even intelligent parents hang back so from using moral stories as part of their children's education? For a very simple reason—because most moralizing stories are bad stories. And they are bad because they are written by professional moralists, people who, with the best intentions in the world, put lies into their stories; that is, who have their eyes so fixed on the moral they are trying to inculcate, that they won't take time and energy to walk around and in and out the long, winding but clear road of truth, but plunge through the underbrush in an attempt at a shortcut, and pretend they've reached their goal when they really are nowhere at all.
>
> They don't care—and, to anyone with any literary feeling at all of the sacredness of truth about human nature, this not caring is sacrilege against the light itself—they simply don't care about making the people in their stories act as people would or could act, so long as they can dangle the moral at the end. But of course since practically everybody, young and old, except professional moralists, does have a keen sense of the sacredness of telling the truth about human nature in stories, by the time such storytellers reach their moral, they haven't anybody left to dangle it before—except other moralists.

The enumeration of arbitrary rules for storytelling is hazardous. Some natural storytellers seem to violate certain of the rules, but they more than compensate by their genuine understanding of children and a spontaneous desire to share an experience. Walter L. Hervey writes:

> The secret of good story-telling lies not in following rules, not in analyzing processes, not even in imitating good models, though all these are necessary, but first of all in being *full*—full of the story and the children; and then from being morally and spiritually up to concert pitch, which is the true source of power in anything. From these come spontaneity; what is within must come out; the story tells itself; and out of your fullness the children receive.

There are, moreover, a number of suggestions to be gleaned from the experience of those persons who have successfully written for or effectively communicated with children.

Children listen attentively to stories that are told with animation and verve. Action highlights character so that there is the emotional impact without which stories never seem altogether convincing. Imagination and color are indispensable ingredients in storytelling. Too exaggerated tonal qualities or gesturing may focus the child's attention more on the unnatural behavior of the storyteller than on the story. A natural manner, heightened by genuine enthusiasm, is always persuasive.

Stories should be true to life and consistent with a child's experiences. Abstractions, allegories, and fantasies usually have small appeal to children of the junior and intermediate ages. "Object talks" are sometimes abstract because attention may be centered more in the object than in the message which the object is intended to illustrate. True-to-life narration needs to avoid giving easy answers to hard questions or quick solutions to difficult problems. The child should not be left skeptical or bewildered.

Story-sermons are effective when they are complete, that is, when they possess—in the Aristotelian sense—a beginning, a middle, and an ending. In other words, the story ought to *move* from an arresting, if not striking, initial situation or problem through a development on to a reasonable and convincing solution. The sequence of action should suggest a physical conflict or a conflict between alternative ideas. There must be conflict of some kind, for without it nothing happens and the child's interest is not sustained. A feeling of suspense or an indecisive situation "holds" the child. All elements which do not contribute to this forward movement should be ruthlessly eliminated, for they deter the story's progress and detract from the story's purpose.

The characters need to be living, breathing persons who act, talk, and think in ways familiar to children. Their conversations are most forceful when they are given in direct dialogue. Instead of talking about characters, the storyteller needs to let them talk for themselves.

Children's understanding of a story is frequently impeded by long and cumbersome sentences or by a series of sentences welded together with conjunctions. A child's vocabulary, of course, is limted, and the child cannot be expected to guess what too many big words may mean. However, this fact should not rule out an occasional use of an unusual word, for children love new and "big" words, but the words should be explained or made clear in context. Flowery phrases and gaudy descriptions mean little to children and hamper the movement of the story.

Many people can read aloud skillfully, but generally in group work, stories are best told without book or notes. When the storyteller has his story well in hand he is better able to maintain the "eye-contact" that enhances the empathy which commands respect and holds attention. Moreover, when a story is well told there is no danger of losing the interest of adults who may be listening in.

Enthusiasm and continued practice produce effectiveness in storytelling. This is true for every storyteller; the art is one which any person may acquire. Nora Archibald Smith has written with discernment:

If one has neither natural adaptation nor experience, still I say, tell the stories; tell the stories; a thousand times, tell the stories! You have no cold, unsympathetic audience to deal with; the child is helpful, receptive, warm, eager, friendly. His whole-hearted interest, his surprise, admiration, and wise comment will spur you on.

Storytelling not only benefits the children; its rewards and satisfactions for the narrator are numerous. Often the pastor, teacher, or parent will discover that he is more ministered unto than ministering. Perhaps through his contact with children he will more fully understand the childlike simplicity, enthusiasm, and integrity which Christ said were needed to enter his kingdom.

C. L. W.

A
Treasury of Story Sermons
for Children

1. THE CHEERFUL HEART

❦

SOLID SUNSHINE

Be of good cheer. JOHN 16:33

I have brought something valuable with me and that is why it is wrapped in tissue paper. No, it is not jewelry. See, it is a piece of coal. Did I hear you say, "I thought you said something valuable"? Yes, and so I did. Coal is one of our most valuable possessions. I am not going to call it coal though, but a name which is better suited to it—*solid sunshine.*

That is what coal really is. Thousands of centuries ago, long before man lived on the earth, this country was covered with vast forests. These flourished in a hot, steamy atmosphere storing in themselves the radiant sunshine in which they basked year in and year out.

As time went on, the forests decayed and sank into the soft, marshy earth, and other forests grew up over them. These in their turn decayed and sank to make room for still more forests. Then as the centuries rolled by, the buried forests underwent a great change and were gradually turned into seams of coal, or as I say solid sunshine.

If you burn this piece of solid sunshine, what happens? Why, of course, it gives out light and heat. It gives up the sunshine it had stored in itself when it was part of a tree basking in the sunshine in the primeval forest. It lets loose sunshine that has been imprisoned millions of years. That is very wonderful, isn't it?

So coal is solid sunshine, and what a precious thing sunshine is. Someday I think clever men will invent a way of storing up all the sunshine that is wasted on the great deserts of the earth, like the Sahara, and send it for use in countries like ours, in the dull, dark days of winter, so that girls and boys, sick folk and old folk will be able to have sunshine all the year round. What a great thing that would be.

Think of all the dark, sad and gloomy spots we could cheer and brighten up if only we had a bit of this solid sunshine always with us. We don't usually put coal on the mantelpiece, but what about finding a little lump of bright shiny solid sunshine to put on the mantelpiece in your room, just to remind you when you wake up in the morning, to take a bit of the other sort of solid sunshine—good cheer—with you downstairs and out into the world wherever there are folk who are sunshine-hungry. "Be of good cheer." Christ, who said this, teaches us that the secret of good cheer is trust in our heavenly Father's love and obedience to his will. Trust and obey, and be a solid sunshine Christian.*

H. Lovering Picken

2   *DO YOU OWN YOUR FACE?*

A merry heart maketh a cheerful countenance.
PROVERBS 15:13

Do you own your face? Think carefully before you answer. Do you? There are many things we call "our own" or "our very own," when we are real sure we own them. They may be the jackknife and marbles or the rabbits or the hair ribbons or rings or dolls. We can sell them, if we wish, or we say we can trade them to some of our boy or girl friends, if we can find anyone who will trade. Sometimes we are glad over our trades, and sometimes we are not.

But there are some things you have that you can't trade and really don't own. Your face is one of them. I see your brown or blue eyes, your straight or pug noses, your rosy cheeks, but you don't own them. Why? Because they belong to other people. They are the ones that have to look at your face, aren't they? Wouldn't it be grand if they might always look as happy and smiling and pleasant as they do now?

Are they always that way? Or do you sometimes look cross when your mother or father asks you to stop your play for a few minutes to do something for them? Perhaps the corners of your mouth turn down, and your forehead wrinkles, your teeth set, a cloud comes over your face, and you look as if you had lost your last friend. My, but you're a sight. You make everyone about you unhappy by looking so much like a storm, and then, too, you make yourself more and more unhappy.

I wish that we might always have a mirror in front of our faces. We would always be happy, and I'll tell you why. We would become awfully tired of looking at ourselves if we weren't looking pleasant. Just try this the next time you begin to get cross. Go right over and look in the mirror. Do you know what will happen? I do, for I've tried it. You'll first lose the frown, then begin to smile a little, then grin, and then burst into a loud and happy laugh. You simply can't keep your face straight. And then the other person in the mirror will laugh

3

back at you. You'll just trade your cross face for a jolly sunshiny one, and you'll wear a smile that will not come off for quite a while.

Would you like to see a smile over twenty-four thousand miles long? One could be that long if everyone would help. You begin smiling and the person next to you begins to smile, and then someone else sees both of you happy and he begins to smile, and then more and more other folks begin to smile, and at last the chain of happy smiles reaches around the world. Laugh, and the world laughs with you.

That's what Gods wants—a twenty-four-thousand-mile smile. He wants everyone in this whole world to be happy. He has placed so many delightful and beautiful things here, and has given us so many good friends, that we would be truly ungrateful if we did not smile and be happy.

Our faces show to others just the kind of folks we are, and let them know quite a bit of what we are thinking. There was once a very famous detective, who could catch robbers and lawbreakers when the other detectives failed. Someone asked him one time just how he was able to do such clever work. He said: "When I am told to find a man, I get his picture, and a mirror, and try to look as much like him as possible. Then I try to think of the things and the places of which he would think. It's easy, for you see I try to look like him. Then I go where I think he would go, and usually catch him."

By keeping our faces bright and happy we can do God's work here ever so much better. He wants us to be just the happiest possible, for he is glad, too, when we are. Let's always wear that bright, happy face that shows others that we know God and that he loves us.

Weldon F. Crossland

3   BRIGHTENING UP THE DARK DAYS

Christ . . . is our life. COLOSSIANS 3:4

Have you ever noticed how the weather affects our dispositions? On bright, sunny days we feel fine. Laughter bubbles from our lips and we greet others with a cheerful "Good morning." But on the days when the sky is overcast and dark rain clouds hang low, we are apt to feel a bit depressed and we allow gloomy and grim expressions to show on our faces.

A shopkeeper in Boston noticed how he ordinarily was low in spirit when the weather was dark and gloomy. But something affected him even more strongly than the weather. It always happened when a certain man walked past his shop. When he saw Phillips Brooks go past his window on his way to Trinity Church, he always felt better. It was as though a ray of sunshine had broken through the mass of dark clouds and his heart was made glad. Phillips Brooks helped that shopkeeper to live a better life with renewed courage and strength.

Phillips Brooks was the minister of Trinity Church, Boston, and one of the outstanding preachers of our country. He was well known and greatly beloved. He won his way into the hearts of many people, young and old, rich and poor. Why were so many people attracted to him?

An artist has helped us to answer this question. The artist, whose name is Augustus Saint-Gaudens, was asked to make a statue of Phillips Brooks. He wondered how he could sculpture the statue so that it might adequately portray the spirit of the great man. Gradually an idea shaped in his mind, and the finished product now stands in front of Trinity Church for all the world to see.

The statue shows Phillips Brooks in his pulpit and directly behind him is the figure of Christ. The hand of Christ rests on the preacher's shoulder. The only satisfactory key to the understanding of this man, thought the artist, is Jesus Christ. Why was that?

The reason is that Phillips Brooks completely dedicated himself to Christ. He did not live to please himself. He felt that he couldn't please himself because he belonged to Christ. He was Christ's man. Whatever Christ desired, he desired, and whatever Christ loved, he loved. He became so closely bound to Christ that the life of Christ became his life. He no longer cared to live a life of his own; he lived the life of Christ. That was what St. Paul meant when he wrote, "Christ . . . is our life."

So it should be with all Christian people. If the spirit of Christ fills our spirit so that we live the life of Christ, we have a source of inspiration, giving us renewed courage and strength, which brightens up even the darkest day. That is what Christ promised us: "He who follows me will never walk in darkness, he will enjoy the light of life" (John 8:12, Moffatt).

Karl H. A. Rest

4   *WHAT DO YOU SAY?*

There are two boys and two girls in this story.

One boy and one girl we will call Brother and Sister Careless.

The other boy and girl we shall name Brother and Sister Courteous.

The Careless children do not say things which the Courteous children say, and the Courteous children do not say the things the Careless children say. Let's listen and find out about this.

The four children go home from school. They are hungry and ask their mothers to prepare a lunch. So the mothers get the food ready as soon as they can and take it to the children. The Careless children say to their mother: "Well, it's about time!" The Courteous children say to their mother, "Thank you!"

Sometimes the children find their parents very busy keeping the home clean and attractive for the family. When it is suggested that the children can help by doing some small task the Careless children say, "Aw, do we have to?" but the Courteous children say, "We want to help, too."

At school, when all four children are feeling cheerful, their teacher asks if they would like to clean the blackboards. The Careless children say, "Oh, okeh." The Courteous children say, "We'll be glad to."

When the children want very much to do something which they have often not been permitted to do, like going to the stores alone, the Careless children say, "Give us a break, will ya?" but the Courteous children say, "Please, may we?"

So you see that the Careless children and the Courteous children do not speak the same language. They live in the same town, go to the same school, and they may even attend the same church. But they say things differently because they think differently. They are different. All through life their names will be Careless or Courteous according to their speech.

What do you say?

Glenn H. Asquith

2. GROWING IN STATURE AND WISDOM

❦

GROWING TALL AND STRAIGHT

And the Lord said to me, "Amos, what do you see?" And I said, "A plumb line." Then the Lord said, "Behold, I am setting a plumb line in the midst of my people Israel."   AMOS 7:7-8 (RSV)

When did you last measure yourself to see how much you had grown? Probably in the kitchen or in your bedroom there is a series of markings and these show your height at different times. That always interests us while we are growing up. But actually this is not the most important thing. What most counts is not how tall you are, but how straight you are.

God is always concerned with quality, not quantity. The Bible tells us that Methuselah lived to be 969 years old, and then he died. Apparently that is about all he ever did! What good is it to live to be 969 if you don't accomplish anything?

The Bible tells us that God is very concerned about how straight we are. He sent his servant Amos into the northern kingdom to preach against the evil things the people were doing. And a part of the message was a vision of a plumb line. Now, a plumb line is a tool that builders use even today. It is simply a heavy weight on the end of a piece of string. A building contractor uses it to measure the accuracy of a wall. By fastening the string at a high point and letting the weight hang down almost to the ground, he has a line that is absolutely straight.

God measures each of us. He wants to be sure we are straight and true. And he gives us a way in which we may measure ourselves. We can measure our lives by the life of our Lord, and so determine whether we are pleasing to God.

Don't measure your life by what someone else is doing. Sometimes that makes us look like shining examples of perfection, but it is not the way God wants us to be measured. If you look at someone else, you may say, "Oh, I don't do the things that he is doing." That may make you quite pleased with yourself. But when we compare our lives with that of Jesus Christ, who was perfect in every respect, then we don't feel so proud of our goodness.

By measuring ourselves according to Jesus, by following him, and by trying to be like him, we shall please God and live lives that will help to build his Kingdom. Then we will be growing tall in height and also straight in character.

William Goddard Sherman

6   *GROWING TOWARD GOD*

Close to the shore of a beautiful lake, away back in the mountains of Maine, there grew a very wonderful pine tree. Its branches reached far and wide, as if trying to drink in more and more of the clear air and bright sunshine. Its top reached up into the sky, as if trying to see what was beyond the fleecy clouds that floated above it. Its trunk was straight and strong, as it had need to be when the cold, northwest winds of winter blew down the lake. The great pine tree was much admired by the people who summered in the cottage close by, and they had named it Monarch.

One day Monarch felt someone digging at its roots, and, looking down, it saw a little spruce tree being planted there. Then the great pine tree rustled in all its branches for very joy. It had been lonely living there alone for so many years; now there would be someone to talk to, and someone to help to grow. The little spruce tree heard the rustling, so when its roots were set, it began to look about to see who its neighbors might be, and it discovered Monarch, the great pine.

"Oh! Oh!" said the little tree. "What a big, big tree! How I should like to be as tall as that pine tree! How much it must see away up there in the sky! I am glad that I am planted close to such a wonderful tree. Perhaps I can grow to be like it, if I try."

That very night, when all was still, the little tree heard a whisper stealing down on the soft, night air. And the voice said, "Little tree. Little tree."

"Yes, dear, big pine," answered the spruce tree. "I am listening to you."

"Little spruce tree," continued the pine, "I am glad that you have come to live near me. You are a pretty little tree, and all the dear children will love you when they come to play in their 'crow's nest,' away up here in my branches. Can I help you in any way?"

"Yes, indeed, you can," replied the spruce. "I have been looking at you for ever so long. What a wonderful tree you are! Tell me, please, how to grow as tall and straight and strong as you."

"That is not a hard thing to tell, but it is a very hard thing to do," murmured the pine. "If you want to grow tall and straight and strong, you must keep looking upward every day, and let nothing bend or break you. You must desire with all your might to become one of the best trees, and then you must grow and grow and grow."

"That I will do," promised the spruce. "I will keep close to you, and every day I will try to grow to be just like you, for I want to be tall and straight and strong."

The days passed by, and every night the little spruce looked carefully to make sure that her trunk was just as straight as the trunk of the pine. Since she had a perfect tree to copy, she grew straight and strong, of course. When the winter came, and the strong winds from the north whistled through the needles of the spruce tree, the pine was just in front of her, and saved her from the force of the wind. At night, when the wind had gone down and all was still again, the big friend would whisper.

"That was a hard breeze, little one, but it is over now, and you have gained strength by fighting it. Now look up and straighten up so that all the bend will be taken out of you. Measure your trunk by mine, if you like." The little tree would try its best, and then, looking up, would thank the Heavenly Father for its good friend and helper.

Finally, after many years, the little tree had grown so tall that her top just reached the lower branches of the pine. How proud she was then as some of her needles actually touched those of the giant tree! She nestled close to the big limb and whispered,

"Oh, dear Monarch, I have so loved to see you away up here. But now that I can touch you and feel your big strong arms, I don't care whether I grow any more or not."

"Tut, tut, little friend of mine," chided the pine tree. "If I had stayed as small as you are now, you would never have been proud to have lived by me and to have called me friend. Surely no one would ever have called me by the beautiful name that the folks who live in the cottage use when they speak of me— Monarch. Indeed, you must not stop growing. I can see much farther than you can. I can breathe much better as I grow higher up. Then, too, I am nearer to the Great and Loving Father when I am doing my best to grow."

"But you get more of the wind and the cold up there," said the spruce tree. "Down here I am sheltered by you."

"That may be," replied the giant pine, "but you cannot give shelter, nor be an example, if you are content to stay down there. Come up, child! Come up."

So the little spruce took courage and pushed ahead until her branches were mingled with those of the pine. Now they could talk together of the beautiful things that they could see around the mountain lake. Then, to her surprise, she found that the pine was still growing—still making sure that she, too, did not bend.

"Aren't you ever going to stop growing?" asked the spruce. "Surely you are big enough now."

But Monarch made answer, "I shall never be big enough, no matter how high I grow to be. I have heard of pine trees that were much taller and larger than I, so I must keep on growing. How could I be an example for you if I stopped reaching up? I must grow for your sake, if for no other reason." Then the spruce loved her old friend all the more, and in her heart she resolved again to keep growing every day, to let nothing bend or break her.

One day, very early in the spring, when the snow was just

13

leaving the ground, the spruce tree was looking down and was thinking of the days when she had been a tiny tree. Suddenly she saw a seedling balsam nestling close to her trunk, and she heard the balsam whisper to the arbutus blossoms on the ground,

"Do you see that big spruce tree away up there? Some day I am going to be tall and straight and strong, just like that spruce tree. You just watch me grow, year by year, until my top reaches those lower branches."

"Well, well!" said the spruce. "Here I am pushing ahead to be like the pine, and that little balsam is trying to be like me. I must grow to be very straight and strong if I am to be an example to that little tree. I cannot stop growing, either, for the balsam will be watching me. The old tree told the truth. I, too, am an example."

So the pine helped the spruce, and sheltered it from the blasts of winter; the spruce helped the balsam, and kept the great drifts of snow from breaking it down; and the balsam spread its tiny branches over the arbutus plants and kept them warm, so that the children might have the joy of finding blossoms there in the spring.

And those who lived in the cottage looked at the four friends —the pine, the spruce, the balsam, and the arbutus—and they learned from them lessons of strength, of beauty, of courage, of helpfulness and of daily striving.

"We, too," they said, "must look upward every day, and let nothing bend or break us. We, too, must measure our strength by One who is greater and stronger than we are. Each of us is an example to others."

Margaret W. Eggleston

7   *OAKS AND SQUASHES*

At some time or other every one of you has probably walked along in some fine, big wood of oak trees. There were the great trunks all about you, so large that two or three boys and girls together could not get their arms all the way around one; and up above were the long branches, with the leaves that made the deep, cool shade. You know that the oak is one of the very finest of all the trees that grow, and that the wood of it is used in a great many sorts of work which people want to be the best. The hardest floors are made of it. Furniture is made of it; pulpits in churches are made of it, and other beautiful things.

And while you walked under the big oaks you looked at the ground and saw a great many little things like this. They were acorns, you say; and you know that out of just such little acorns the tremendous oak trees grow.

But what I want you to think about today is this: it takes a long, long while for an acorn to grow into an oak. It will certainly make an oak if you give it time enough, but if you want to plant something that will sprout right up and make a big appearance quickly, you just cannot have an oak.

Of course, there are some things that do grow quickly. Do you remember how a squash vine looks? You plant the seed and after a few weeks there is the big vine, trailing all over the ground, and presently you have the yellow squashes on it. You can almost see them grow, but when they are grown they are only squashes after all. And if you wanted to build a house you certainly would not want to build it out of soft, squashy squashes, and the next week have it come squashing down.

God works with people, too, in much the same way in which he works with squashes and oaks. If all you want to be is a squash you can grow into one very soon, and without much pains. But if you want to be an oak, you must remember that God will have to take a long while to make you anything so big and fine.

I wonder if any boys and girls here belong with the squashes. If ever you get into the way at school of thinking more of making a large showing than you do of honest work, and if you go skimming over things just because you know you can rattle them off that day, even if you forget them the next, then you know that even if you look big you really are only a squash after all.

Sometimes we wish we could hurry along and get to what we think are more interesting things. We wish we could finish school and grow up. We want to get through our lessons just as quickly as we can and have all the rest of the time left for play. We get tired of having to be made to learn so much, and to do so many things. But it all begins to look different when we think of what we want to be. If we want to be like the great oaks, solid and strong, we must remember that God must take a great deal of pains with us and must keep on making us grow for a long, long time.

Walter Russell Bowie

8   *KEEPING THE TANK FULL*

The day we bought our first automobile was a great day in our family. It was many years ago, but I remember it well. I remember, too, many experiences we had with that early model automobile. Those experiences were the kind we could not have today with our beautiful and powerful cars. You would have to have one of those early cars, one of the first automobiles, if you want to have the fun—and trouble—we had. Let me tell you one thing that happened to us.

On the day of our first ride in our automobile, Father stopped to get gas. The man filled the tank, checked the oil and water, and smilingly said "Thank you" when Father paid him. Mother had been sitting quietly in the back seat during all this. As we started off she asked, "What did he do?"

"He put gas in the car," I answered.

Mother had another question: "Why?"

"We used all the gas we had and needed to buy more."

She thought about that for a while and then said: "Oh, I thought that when you bought one of these cars it just went on running and that you didn't have to do anything else to it."

We laughed and told her that we would need to keep adding gas and oil if the car was to keep running. That worried Mother, for she thought of how much it would cost to have the car. It would have been so much better if its purchase price was all it would ever cost to keep it.

Mother learned something that day and so did her son. I learned that you have to keep on taking care of anything you have. If you buy a little dog, for instance, you have to pay something to keep it. You will have to pay for its food, and you will have also to pay something in time and effort to give it exercise and keep it healthy. Indeed, if you want your little dog to be a real friend, you have to spend time playing with it and being its friend.

All this, of course, is true also of our own bodies and minds.

They do not grow straight and strong and good unless we take time to help them. It costs something even to be liked by other people. We must love them and show our love by doing friendly things and by saying friendly words.

We come to church and church school, and we ask God to keep our lives full of the power we need to serve him in every way and in every place he needs us. Loving God requires that we give him generously of ourselves.

Robert E. Keighton

9   *THE WHAT FAMILY*

Once Jesus said, "You shall love the Lord your God . . . with all your mind" (Luke 10:27, RSV). Have you any idea what he meant? Thinking about this reminded me of a story.

For a long time Do-You-Know-What was looking around for a wife. When at last he met What-Do-You-Think, it seemed as if she were just the girl for him. It was love at first sight. So they were married and that was the beginning of the What family.

Their first child was a big, sturdy boy. They named him "What." What else could they have named him? He was always asking, "What?"—"What shall we make now? What shall we do next?" Being called "What" just suited him.

The next child was a smaller boy, but oh, what a mouth he had! They named him "Why." What else could they have named him, because he was always asking, "Why?"—why this and why that, from morning till night. Being called "Why" just suited him.

The third child was a long, lanky fellow. They named him "Where." What else could they have named him, because he

The What Family

was always asking, "Where?"—"Where are we going today? Where will we be tomorrow?" Being called "Where" just suited him.

You can imagine what kind of family it was with What asking what, Why asking why, and Where asking where. Sometimes it sounded like a madhouse.

"Do you know what?" said Do-You-Know-What. "*What* will become of us? All these questions are driving me crazy. These boys will never get anywhere."

"Do you know what I think?" said What-Do-You-Think. "That is just the reason why they *will* get somewhere!"

At last the time came for the boys to go out to seek their fortunes. They looked around until they came to a factory. "Let's go in and see if we can find something to do," they said.

The man there looked at What and said, "Name, please." "What." "What?" "What—that is my name, sir."

"Father's name?" said the man. What said, "Do-You-Know-What." "Mother's name?" said the man. "What-Do-You-Think," said What.

"What can you do?" "I can ask, 'What?—what shall we do now? what shall we do next?'"

"All right," said the man, "we'll put you in the Main Office, where we plan things."

The man came to Why. "Name, please?" "Why." "Why?" "Why—that is my name, sir." "What can you do?" "I can ask, 'Why?—why this and why that.' I ask a great many questions." "All right, I'll put you in the Research Department, where we find out things."

Then he came to Where. "Name, please?" "Where." "Where?" "Where is my name, sir." "What can you do?" "I can ask,

'Where?—where do we go next?' " "All right, we'll put you in the Shipping Room, where we send out our products." He was a wise man because he put those boys just where they could use what they had.

I haven't time to tell you all about the What boys, but they did well, for they used what they had. What, in the Main Office, became the father of all managers and businessmen and secretaries. Why, in the Research Department, became the father of all lawyers, ministers, and politicians. Where, in the Shipping Room, became the father of all pioneers and scientists and explorers like Christopher Columbus.

Questions *do* at times drive parents to distraction, but ask ahead. God can use a mind that asks honest questions. Jesus also said, "Ask, and it will be given you; seek, and you will find" (Luke 11:9, RSV).

Kenneth Brakeley Welles

10   *WHY WERE YOU BORN?*

This is why I was born. JOHN 18:37 (MOFFATT)

God gave every one of you a sense of curiosity. He put you into a world that is full of wonders, and he expects you to think about it, to wonder about it, and to ask questions about it.

In school you have probably been told that you should ask these questions about everything: Who? What? When? Where? and Why? If you ask those questions about anything, you will know almost everything about it. They are all important questions, but I think the most important is the last one, why?

Let's ask that question about you. Why did God make you? Why were you born?

Why Were You Born?

Christmas is the time when we think especially about the birth of Jesus. Our text says that Jesus knew why he came into the world. Even when he was twelve years old he knew he had to be about his Father's business. So, it isn't too early for you to ask this question about yourself. Why was I born? For what reasons am I here?

Some very surprising things come to mind when you ask yourself these questions. You might have been born in Africa, or China, or Iceland. Or you might have been born with a different colored skin. There are many might-have-beens. But these didn't happen. You were born in America and many of you in this beautiful community. Why?

The world will continue to exist for a long time, and God wants the world to be good. He wants it to be a better world in your home and your city and your country. That's why he put you here.

God wants to keep the best things from your parents' lives, so he gave you to them that they might teach you. Your father and mother helped to build this church. God wants to keep the church alive, so he put you here.

God put you into the world so that the good which was in the world before your birth would not come to an end. You were born that the truth of the past might continue to live. You were born that yesterday might not pass away forever.

You were born for today, too. The Apostle Paul said to the people of his day, "Ye are our epistle written in our hearts, known and read of all men" (2 Corinthians 3:2). Boys and girls, you are letters of God for the world to read. Many people do not read the Bible. The only message they have is in you. You are Christ's letters to the world.

You were born also for tomorrow. One night a little boy

named Tommy had a strange dream. He dreamed that many persons visited him. The doctor, who was worn out after caring for the sick, came and asked Tommy to take over his practice. The lawyer came. He said he had finished practicing law and asked Tommy if he would continue his work. Then the town drunkard came. He said he was tired of being laughed at and wanted Tommy to take his place. Others came also. There were a banker, a teacher, a minister, and the town liar. Each said he was counting on Tommy to take his place and live his life.

That sounds like a strange dream, but after all that is exactly what happens. Every boy takes the place of some man and every girl takes the place of some woman. Do you think God gave you birth that you might one day become the town drunkard or the town liar?

Why were you born? God wants you to save the good out of yesterday, to live for him today, and to grow into his man or woman tomorrow. You are mighty important. God has meaning for your life. Don't disappoint God!

Peter H. Pleune

11   *THE DOOR OF A DAY*

Look at the page of a calendar. There are the figures: 1, 2, 3, and on to 31. Each number stands for a day. Suppose that, instead of going to bed at night on the eleventh day of the month, you could walk up to the calendar, find a small latch next to the figure 12, open the door of that day and walk right in! Perhaps there would be a long corridor with partitions marked Hours and Minutes, and you could walk right down that hall until you had passed the last section of the 60th minute of the 24th hour.

The Door of a Day

What do you suppose you would find inside a day?

You would surely find Adventure. Not the kind that you read about in books called "thrillers," but real Adventure, nevertheless. Anything that you are about to do which has never been done before is an Adventure. Every day is new and no one has ever lived it before. Anything could happen! There will be new people to meet, new things to do, new surprises.

And you would find Learning. A day is much better than a schoolroom for teaching. Maybe you will not learn history dates or arithmetic or rules of grammar, but you will learn about life and the world around you.

Growth, also, will be in the day. If you could use a delicate instrument, you would find that your body is a trifle larger at the end of the day than it was at the beginning. Boys and girls have many days of growth ahead of them. But not only the body grows. The mind and the soul grow, too.

Love is always somewhere along the path of a day. We love our parents, playmates, brothers and sisters, and others. It is Love that makes the day full of sunshine, no matter what the weather may be.

Do not miss Worship. If a boy or girl thinks about God and longs to be near him and to be like him, that is Worship. When you worship you feel that God has entered the door of the day along with you.

There are so many things to be found in one day. You can name dozens yourself. Every day is so full, and every day is so different that we dare not waste even one.

"Oh, if only I could pull open the door of a day," you may be saying to yourself. But you do! You have! How? Well, we said, suppose instead of going to sleep at night you could just walk right up to the next day and go in. That is exactly what you do when you go to sleep at the end of the day. While you are sleeping, God throws open a new day for you and you awaken to find yourself in it. You are in a day at this very moment. Have you found all the wonderful things put there for you?

Glenn H. Asquith

12   *RULES FOR LIVING*

Scripture: EXODUS 20:1-17

Of course, we have to have rules by which to live. None of us can do just as he pleases. Naturally there are times when we feel that we could get along better without rules. Sometimes we say that rules take the fun out of life. But everybody has to live by some rules. There are some rules that are the same for everybody, for children and grownups, for teachers and ministers, and even for the President of the United States. These rules are for everyone, everywhere.

These rules ought to be good rules, if they are for everybody. And they are good rules, because they were made by God. We call them the Ten Commandments.

The Ten Commandments are very old. God gave them long ago to people who lived in tents and in a far corner of the world. Those people had no automobiles, no airplanes, no television sets. Everything about them and everything about us seems different. How can rules for them and rules for us be the same? They are the same because rules are for persons, not things. Things change, but people don't change. These are rules for living in any year, thirty-five hundred years ago, today, or five thousand years from now. These rules are good ones, and we don't need new ones.

But these rules, called the Ten Commandments, seem to be mostly rules about what not to do. The word "don't" is never very popular. Sometimes you may feel that whenever you want to do something, someone says "don't do it." But suppose that you heard only the word "do." Wouldn't you get tired of that word after a time?

We need both words, "don't" and "do." When God says, "Don't tell a lie," he means also, "Do tell the truth." And that is the best way not to tell a lie, isn't it? Every rule has a "do" side as well as a "don't" side. If you pay attention to the "do" side, you won't have to worry about the "don't" side.

The Ten Commandments always mean what they say, and you cannot change the words around or substitute other rules for them. A little girl memorized the Ten Commandments. Her mother tried to see that she understood what each of the commandments meant. Then one day she found that the cookie jar was half empty. So she called to her daughter and said, "I believe this cookie jar must know all about the Ten Commandments because it surely heard us going over them again and again. Now, suppose that the cookie jar could talk. Which commandment would the cookie jar say had been broken?" The little girl hesitated for a moment. Then she said, "I think the cookie jar would say, 'Let the little children come unto me.' "

Clever little girl, wasn't she? But, seriously, you can never do that. You cannot replace the words of the Bible with your own words, no matter how good they may seem. It is impossible to replace "steal" with the words "help yourself." When God makes a rule he says what he means and he means what he says.

God gave us only Ten Commandments. Ten were enough, because they cover everything. Men have made many rules since then. If all the laws man has made were printed in books and all the books were brought into this room, I'm sure there wouldn't be much space left. But God made only ten rules. We can remember ten. And we ought to remember that they are good rules and that they never will go out of date. We ought also to remember that they mean what they say and not what we might want them to say.

The Ten Commandments are God's rules for living. He knows what is best for us. We show our love for God when we keep his rules in our own lives.

Peter H. Pleune

13   *AN EFFECTIVE TEAM*

Striving together. PHILIPPIANS 1:27

While visiting a Labrador missionary I learned a very valuable lesson from a team of dogs. The missionary has found that a dog team and a native sled, called a "komatik," is an excellent means of getting from place to place over the frozen snow when he holds church services in a distant village or goes to some isolated spot to visit a sick or lonely person.

One clear day, when the sun shone strongly on the dazzling snow and the air was so still and crisp that a shout could be heard for miles, we prepared for a trip of about twenty-five miles. The missionary thought that this would be a good opportunity to "break in" two young dogs which had never before been harnessed. They were beautiful puppies, full of energy and fun, but they had not yet become part of the team. They offered no resistance when the simple shoulder harness was put over their heads and a long thong, called a "trace," was passed between the legs of each and then fastened with all the other traces to a ring on the front of the komatik. Their inexperience, however, was obvious the moment we started to move.

The older dogs knew exactly what to do as they set off eagerly across the unmarked snow, but the young ones seemed to have ideas of their own. Both of them bolted to the right with such undisciplined energy that they pulled the sled off its course and soon had themselves and all the other dogs rolling in a confused heap.

With great patience and many words of encouragement, the missionary calmed the yelping team and, when all the traces were untangled, he tried again, urging the new members of the team to follow the example of the older dogs. For a few hundred yards the sled moved fairly well, but then the two puppies saw something moving among the low evergreen trees along the side of the lake. This time they ran off to the left, and again they created a great deal of confusion and brought the sled to a stop.

After several more mishaps, the young dogs discovered for themselves that they must co-operate with the pack and follow the trail of the older and wiser dogs if they hoped to get to the end of the run and to the meal which always awaits them as a reward when the run is well finished.

I learned a great deal that day as I ran behind the team or rode the komatik. All of us, while we are young, must learn to become members of some team or other. The team may be the family, it may be the community in which we live, or it may be the church. Whichever it be, there is always somebody older and wiser than we with whom we must co-operate if we wish to attain any worth-while goal. Like the young puppies, we may first of all be inclined to dash off to the right or to the left, thereby decreasing the efficiency of the whole group and proving ourselves to be quite inexperienced. But, sooner or later, we must come to the understanding that, though we may have more actual strength and endurance than the older people with whom we work, yet they are the ones who, through long years of experience in harness and many trips over the trail, can best judge the actual direction in which we should travel. They can best teach us the basic rules of vital team membership.

Walter C. Sellars

14 *BETTER THAN BEAUTY*

Man looketh on the outward appearance, but the Lord looketh on the heart. 1 SAMUEL 16:7

Almost everyone has said, "I wish I were more beautiful." Perhaps you have said that very thing. Few people are completely satisfied with their appearance. Even the most attractive persons wish to be more beautiful.

Boys, perhaps, do not long for the same kind of beauty that girls want, but most boys wish to be big and strong, to look like an all-star athlete, and to be tall and muscular.

There was once an attractive little girl who wished to be beautiful. Finally she persuaded her father to have an artist paint her portrait. She knew that the artist could skillfully alter those features which she considered ugly and make her beautiful.

So the little girl went every day to the artist's studio. There she sat quietly while the artist worked on the portrait. Each day she became more excited, for she knew that in the portrait she would be truly beautiful.

The artist did his work skillfully and well. He, too, hoped his young model would be pleased with his portrait. Then at last the day came when the picture was complete. The artist thought the portrait was one of his finest. He invited the little girl and her father to come to the studio. Carefully the artist removed the cloth veil that covered the picture. For a long time the father stared at the picture. He said nothing, as if he could not believe his eyes. The artist and the little girl watched him anxiously and waited for him to speak.

Instead of a smile, sadness came into the father's face. "Take this picture away," he cried. "This is not my daughter. You have made her too beautiful."

The little girl began to cry. She was so proud of the picture of the beautiful girl. Now she was greatly disappointed. Her father gently took her into his arms. He hugged her and kissed her. "I love you as you are," he said. "Why should I want a painting of you? I think you are the most beautiful girl in the whole world."

The little girl was never more happy. She knew that her father's love was better than beauty. He loved her because she belonged to him. He saw a beauty which even the artist could not know. He loved her for what she was and not for what she wished to be.

Do you wish to be beautiful, or handsome, or strong? Then do what you can. Eat, sleep, exercise, keep clean. That's fine. But remember this. Most of us want to be more beautiful because we think that will make us more happy or more popular. What we forget is that love is better than beauty. God, our Father, sees us as we are and loves us, for we are his children and we belong to him. "The Lord seeth not as man seeth; for man looketh on the outward appearance, but the Lord looketh on the heart."

Galen E. Hershey

15   *THE AX AND THE SAW*

I heard two boys talking about church school. One was saying, "What's the use of giving us all these things to learn?"

"Yes," said the second boy, "kid stuff."

The first boy said: "If only they would give us something big and important and different to do! We'd be glad to do that."

Here, then, is a story for those boys, and perhaps for the rest of us.

Once there was an ax and a saw. It was noon in the woods and the men were eating their lunch. The ax and the saw were both resting beside the stump of a tree. The ax was a beautiful one, with a broad, sharp, shining blade and a handle polished smooth as glass by the woodman's hand. And the saw was finely tempered, with a hundred teeth all sharp and straight. If you looked along them, you would find them like a line of well-drilled soldiers, not one out of place.

The ax and the saw were talking about their master. The ax said: "He likes me best. I take such big bites. I make the great chips fly. But you take such little bites. No wonder they call your bites dust—sawdust."

The saw didn't say much, but just grinned until you could see all its teeth. Then the woodman came and took the ax.

"I told you so," said the ax. "He likes me best."

The man started trimming branches on a great tree. "Slash, slash, chop, chop" went the ax, and the great chips flew. With every few chops a branch was cut from the trunk. "See that," boasted the ax to the saw, "you couldn't do that. You can't make the big chips fly. You can only make dust. I wonder the master bothers with you at all."

But the saw only grinned and showed his hundred teeth. The man started on the great trunk of the tree with the ax. "Look at that," boasted the ax, as a great chip flew. "You can't do that big stuff with your small teeth."

The man laid down the ax. "That's about all the ax can do," he said. Now it's my turn, thought the saw. Big things must be done little by little.

The man took the saw and another man came. They pulled it back and forth across the tree in the cut the ax had made. Sawdust poured out until it formed little piles at the men's feet.

As the saw worked, it said quietly, in a very different tone from the loud boast of the ax, " 'Precept upon precept, precept upon precept, line upon line, line upon line, here a little, there a little.' " Steadily it worked, each tooth taking its own little bite as it passed through the wood.

The tree began to sway and a shiver went up the trunk. "Heads up," shouted the men, "timber!" And with a mighty crash, the tree came tumbling to the ground.

The man mopped his brow and looked down at the saw. "When you have a big thing to do, you must do it little by little," he said.

Kenneth Brakeley Welles

16   *GOD'S SCALES*

I am sure that you have all seen pictures of those old-fashioned scales that were used years ago to weigh the farmer's grain or the merchant's oil or the spices that were brought by the caravans into the cities of Palestine. These scales were suspended, or held in the middle, while the scoop at each end swung free. Then, a weight was placed in one side, and the goods to be weighed were heaped into the other side until the scales balanced perfectly.

One day as Jesus talked to a large crowd upon a Judean hillside, he showed them the largest pair of scales that have ever been seen, before or since, for in them he weighed everything in the world. Let me tell you about it.

He must have hung the huge scales from the Milky Way, for there was nothing on earth high enough to hold them. On one side he began to put all the things within sight of the crowd on the hillside. He took the olives from the trees on the slope near by; he took the herd of sheep grazing in the meadow at the foot of the hill; he took all the armor of the Roman soldiers at Jerusalem and piled it into the scales. He reached across the Mediterranean Sea and took the libraries of Alexandria; he reached across the years and the oceans and took all the United States' gold from the storehouse at Fort Knox, Kentucky; he took the jewels from all the Fifth Avenue stores in New York City; he took the bridge from the Golden Gate in San Francisco. All the ivory and all the forests of mahogany from the heart of Africa were heaped upon the mountain of wonderful things, and, by and by, he had everything valuable from every land and every age placed in the left-hand side of the balance. And the people stared in amazement, and said one to another, "There is nothing left to put in the other side of the scales!"

But Jesus knew better, for, looking about him, he took the person nearest him, perhaps just a little child, and placed him in the right-hand side of the scales. And lo, even as the people looked, the scales began to waver. The left-hand side quivered and slowly but surely began to rise in the air until it was tipped at a precarious angle, and all the beautiful things were in danger of spilling out. Then Jesus said to them, "What shall it profit a man, if he shall gain the whole world, and lose his own soul, or what shall a man give in exchange for his soul?" (Mark 8:36-37) He showed them that the soul of one person is more important than everything else in the world.

You see, all of the things that Jesus had put in the left-hand balance were things that are beautiful only for a few years, while we are living on this little earth—perhaps sixty, seventy, or even ninety years—but the thing that he had put in the right-hand balance was a human soul that lasts, not only for the sixty or ninety years of this life, but for the millions of years of beauty and doing in the life to come.

If you are ever tempted to think that it is more important to get money, or to have jewelry or cars, or to travel, or to be popular, than it is to take care of your soul, remember what Jesus said. He said that your soul will outweigh the whole world.

We take care of our souls by doing every day the thing we know Jesus would want us to do, by loving God, and by being kind to all his children on earth. When you do these things, you will never have anything to worry about; you will be on the right side—the safe side—of the scales.

Marian Walter Gannaway

17   *WHAT'S MY NAME?*

I was born in Bethlehem, where Jesus was born; but I was born a thousand years before Jesus. My father's name was Jesse, and Boaz and Ruth were my great-grandparents. I was the youngest of seven sons. What's my name?

When I was a boy I became a shepherd and looked after a flock of sheep. While caring for my father's sheep I sometimes had to fight bears and lions in order to protect the lambs.

Saul was the king of Israel during my youth. At times when he became very sad his servants would suggest that I play the harp for him. While watching the sheep I often practiced on my harp and in time I acquired much skill. When I was taken before the great king and played my harp, the king was pleased. What's my name?

After I had grown up I wrote many songs. Some of these became sacred music of the Jewish people. These are called Psalms. One of them begins like this:

> The Lord is my shepherd, I shall not want;
> He makes me lie down in green pastures.
> He leads me beside still waters;
> He restores my soul. (Psalm 23:1-3, RSV)

What's my name?

While I was still quite young, I took food to my brothers who were fighting in the king's army against the Philistines. Among the Philistines there was a man of great size, named Goliath. This giant challenged any Israelite soldier to fight him. But none would accept his dare. I asked the king if he would let me fight him. So I took a satchel in which I had placed five smooth stones and a sling, and I went forward to meet Goliath. I put a stone into the sling and sent it whizzing toward the forehead of the giant. He fell to the ground. Because I had defeated the giant I became very popular with the king. He placed me at the head of his armies. I was so successful in leading the armies that

What's My Name?

I became very popular with the people, more popular than the king himself. The king grew jealous and sought to destroy me. I had to flee from the king. What's my name?

The king's son, Jonathan, was my friend. His soul was knit to my soul and he loved me as he loved himself. We helped each other in many ways. After Saul, the king, died, I became king of Israel. I moved the capital of the government of Israel from Hebron to Jerusalem, where I desired to build a great temple for God. So I set to the task of collecting materials for building, but the temple was completed only after my son, Solomon, became king.

I had a great trust in God and I tried to be a man after God's own heart. Sometimes I did wrong, but I repented for my sins and God forgave me. In spite of my faults and my sins, I desired in my heart to be always loyal to God. What's my name?

My name is David.

Herman G. McCoy

3. COMPANIONABLE HABITS

❦

THE WONDERFUL HOUSE

Once upon a time a boy was given a wonderful house. It was heated from top to bottom with a hot-water system, it had telephones in every room, all connecting with a central office, and it was filled with wonderful devices for the convenience and pleasure of the owner. The most remarkable thing about the house was the picture gallery at the top. It was finished with a dome, and on the walls were hung beautiful paintings and tapestries, new and old. There were blank spaces on the walls, and the boy was promised that if he wished, the finest artists in the world would come and fill these vacant places with their work. The gentleman who gave the boy this princely gift made only one condition: that he should take good care of his house. "By and by," said he, "I am coming around to see what you have done with it."

Wouldn't you think that the boy would take the very best care of such a house as that? But, do you know? He grew careless and let his house get out of repair. One day he had a lot of other boys in, and they romped all over the house and left their dirty finger-marks everywhere; but the worst of all was that his beautiful art gallery was soiled with smoke and dirt so that it was almost ruined. When his generous friend came to visit him, he was shocked to find how the house had been used. But he did not take his gift back; he had the house thoroughly cleaned, the paintings restored, and new ones replaced those that were damaged beyond repair; then he gave the boy another chance to see if he would not take better care of his house.

I see that some of you have already guessed my parable. The wonderful house which God gives to each one of us is this body of ours; the hot-water system which heats the body is made up of our arteries and veins filled with warm blood; the electric connections in every room are the nerve system centering in the brain; and the dome at the top of the house is the mind where the imagination and memory paint more wonderful pictures than ever artist hung upon his easel. How careless we are with our wonderful houses! And when we welcome evil thoughts and evil imaginations, it is like putting dirty hands upon the walls and defacing the pictures in our art gallery. But God treats us as the generous man treated his young friend. He will come in and clean our hearts and purify our thoughts and give us another chance. There is nothing in this world more wonderful than your body except your mind. May God help us to take good care of this house in which we dwell.

Edward MacArthur Noyes

19 *AWAITING THE TOUCH OF SUN AND RAIN*

A seed is an unpromising, hopeless-looking thing. Take a carrot or radish or lettuce seed from the little store package and look at it carefully. See how dried up it is, and how small! It looks as lifeless as a pebble, Yet, within that seed are all the possibilities of the full-grown carrot or radish or lettuce plant.

Set that seed in the ground in the early springtime and there it will quietly lie awaiting the coming of warm spring sunshine and good spring rains. Then the life stirs sleepily within the seed's husk. The shell-like covering breaks apart, and tiny sprouts reach toward the sky, and little roots probe into the soil. The lifeless, hopeless-appearing seed was really alive all along. It had been simply waiting for the proper conditions it needed for growth, awaiting the touch of sun and rain.

People are like seeds. This is especially true of the very young people. They sometimes seem hopeless, absolutely impossible. Yet within us all there are good possibilities slumbering, like life within a seed. And those possibilities are awaiting the touch of good influences before they can sprout and grow.

One spring day, before the War between the States, a poorly dressed boy appeared at the door of Worthy Taylor, a successful farmer in Portage County, Ohio. The youngster asked the farmer for work, and although Mr. Taylor knew nothing about the lad, excepting his name, Jim, he gave him a job. Jim spent the summer working hard, cultivating the growing crops and helping in the harvest, bringing in the cows from distant fields for morning and evening milking, and cutting wood for the farmhouse stoves. He slept in the haymow and ate in the farm kitchen.

Jim formed a strong liking for Worthy Taylor's daughter. Later this affection turned to love. But Jim was refused permission to marry the girl. Her father told the boy that his prospects were too poor. He had no money, no reputation, and no apparent talents. So Jim took his few belongings, stuffed them into his old carpetbag, and went away.

Thirty-five years came and went. One day Mr. Taylor, now

an old man, tore down his barn to make space on the farm lot for a new one. Far up on the rafters above the haymow he found where that hired farmhand Jim had carved his name— James A. Garfield. At that very moment James A. Garfield was President of the United States of America!

Worthy Taylor was no encouragement to the hidden possibilities within young Jim Garfield. But other people awakened the best in him so that an unlikely appearing farm lad grew into a great servant of the American people.

Thomas Edison, when a small boy, was thought by his teachers to be too stupid to learn. They told his mother that he was a hopeless case. But she believed in him and encouraged his lively imagination. Occasionally others saw a flash of genius in young Tom's curiosity about the nature of things and his ability to experiment with new ideas. Friends inspired him, trusted him, expected great things from him, and cheered him on, until he became one of the world's most distinguished inventors, giving us the electric light, the phonograph, moving pictures, and made unnumbered other contributions to our comfort and happiness.

Nobody would have given Peter, James and John, or any of the other apostles a ghost of a chance of becoming worldrenowned saints, towering spiritual leaders of the human race. They were very ordinary people, and sinners rather than saints. Then Jesus came, like springtime, among them. Under his influence their little, hidden possibilities for splendid character and great discipleship sprouted and grew.

Wherever you find greatness you can be certain that once upon a time it was no more than a tiny seed-like possibility, lying hidden in a life. It grew because some wholesome, good influences fell upon it, like warm sunshine and spring rains, helping it to grow.

It is clear, then, that one thing we need if we are to become the best people we can possibly be is to expose ourselves to the most wholesome influences. Choose the finest of friends, people whose lives will bring out the best within you. Read the most inspiring books. Frequent the places, such as Sunday school and church, that make you feel cleaner and better. And, above all, live always in the awareness of God's nearness to you and his blessing upon you. Such influences will cause seeds of good within you to grow.

Moreover, not only do we need to expose ourselves to the best influences, but we should *be* such influences. We have two roles to play in this drama of life. Sometimes we play the part of growing seeds, and at other times we act like sunshine and rain. We are influenced, but we also are influencers. There are some people whose best possibilities will never sprout and spring up unless we help them as the smiling sun and gentle spring rains encourage the growth of garden seeds.

In 1805, at a council of Indian chiefs of the Six Nations, a white missionary delivered a splendid sermon, appealing to the Indians to become Christians. When he was through, one of the Indian leaders, Chief Red Jacket, quietly arose and replied, "Brother, we have been told that you have been preaching to the white people of this place. These people are our neighbors. We are acquainted with them. We will wait a little while and see what effect your preaching has upon them. If we find it does them good, makes them honest, and less disposed to cheat Indians, then we will consider again what you have said." The great chief was willing that the influence of Christians should fall upon his people. If their example was kindly and good, like warm spring sunshine and gentle spring rains, he knew the tiny seeds of Christian faith planted in Indian hearts would grow.

We are all living in a world where people's minds and hearts have been sown with some little thoughts of God and some small knowledge of Christ. If our lives are warm with the love of God and as refreshing as a shower, we shall help those seeds to grow, making the earth at last into the Garden of God.

Harold E. Kohn

20   *WHAT CAME FROM THE BULB*

When bulbs are put into the ground, we know pretty well what will come up in the spring, unless indeed the labels have been mixed; then we may get a surprise. But if we really know them, we are sure that out of the crocus bulb we shall not get a daffodil. The same seed always gives the same flower. But though they are always of the same kind, there are differences. Those that have been cared for and have had good fertlizer given them are generally more beautiful, and sometimes the gardener himself gets surprises in a color or form which he did not expect.

I want to tell you of some truly remarkable things that came from one particular bulb, planted with a special kind of fertilizer, in what seemed to be rather unpromising soil.

It was a very dirty and untidy house in which it was planted. The man who lived there had fallen into rather bad ways, and was more fond of spending his time in the public-house than at home. I think it was because of this, at least partly, that his wife had become careless and untidy, and that made the house unpleasant, so that the man was less inclined still to spend his evenings there. Then, when the mother does not care, the children forget to wash, and their clothes need mending. Altogether, it was not a nice home.

But one day, a friend of the man, who was sorry about all this drinking and dirtiness, gave him the bulb and asked him to put it into a pot, and see if he could not grow a fine plant for the flower-show which was to be held later on. It was a friendly thing to do, so the man found a pot, filled it with earth and set the bulb. After a time the little green shoot pushed its way through the surface; as it grew the children loved to watch it, the friend would call to see it, and the mother and father became more interested in it. They found a little table and set it in the window. Soon the bud began to form, and at last the beautiful yellow flower unfolded, and seemed to shine like a light in the dingy and disordered room.

Then the contrast between the bright clean flower and the dirty window struck the woman. "I'll clean that window," she thought, and soon the light came through the pane as it had not been able to do for a long time. But the clean window and the stronger light made her notice how untidy the other things round about it were. "My!" she said, "those curtains are grubby; I must clean and mend them too." So the curtains were washed and mended, and when the father came home, he could not help noticing the difference. "Hello, mother," he said. "What have you been doing?" But as he looked, he saw what a rickety old table the flower stood upon, and how a very little push might upset it and the flower together. "I'll mend that before I go out," he said, and so he did. When he had finished, he began putting some of the rest of the furniture straight, and then it was too late to go to the public-house that night. But it struck him that he had had a much better evening than usual. The friend came in the next night, and admired the flower and the way they had arranged it, and the man thought he would give the flower all the attention he could to make a good appearance at the show.

Well, I cannot stop to tell you how it all happened, but one thing led to another and each new clean and tidy thing made them see something else to be made better, until the man had quite got out of the habit of going to the public-house and the mother had cleaned not only the whole house but the children and herself. Meanwhile the friend kept coming, and asked the man to meet other friends where they were talking about better things than drinking and gambling. After a time, they grew to like cleaning up and making things as beautiful as they could, and, best of all, the man came to see that a good home was something better than he could get anywhere else.

So, you see, out of that bulb came very many more things than its own yellow petals, and the name of the fertilizer that helped so much is fellowship or friendship.

This is not only true, and very good in itself, but it is a kind of picture of what Jesus so often does in ourselves. I am afraid our hearts and minds are frequently very much like that house; we have got into bad ways of thinking, of feeling and of behaving generally. We need cleaning up and putting straight, and especially we need to get rid of the grime on our windows so that the light of God can shine through into our hearts. It is difficult for it to come in when between us and God there are so many silly, selfish and wrong thoughts.

But sometimes Jesus plants a beautiful true word in us. He

described himself as a sower of seed, and the seed, he explained, was the word of God. The Bible is full of these seed-words, but we so often let them stay shut up between the covers, like grains in a sack; they have to be in ourselves before their real meaning grows like the plant.*

Will Reason

21   *THE BOY WHO HATED TO WEAR RUBBERS*

"I hate rubbers," scolded Bobby, "and I don't want to carry an umbrella." Then, turning toward his father, Bobby added, "I'll be glad when I grow up and will not have to mind anybody."

"Did you ever hear of anybody who did not have to mind somebody?" his father asked.

"Well, you don't have to, do you?"

"I surely do," Father replied. "How long do you suppose I could work in the office if I didn't follow Mr. Black's suggestions?"

"I never thought of that," returned Bobby. He stopped scowling and his face brightened a little. "What about the farmer? He can do just about as he wants, can't he?"

"I'm afraid he can't," said Father. "He must be obedient to nature. When God says that it is time to plant, he must obey. When God says that it is time to harvest, he must go into the fields. And he has to raise the foods that people want. You might say that he has to mind his customers."

"Well," said Bobby triumphantly, "I know somebody who can do just as he pleases. He's the President."

"The President has the highest office in our country and most people honor and obey him. But he is elected by the people and he is their servant. He must obey the wishes of millions of people. There are times when the President and his helpers are not sure what is the right thing to do, so he prays to God and asks for guidance. That's how he knows what is best for our country."

"Then he must be obedient to God, mustn't he?"

A few moments later Bobby and his father walked down the sidewalk. Bobby's rubbers kept his shoes dry and his umbrella protected his clothes. "Daddy, I'm glad our President loves God. I guess that is why he knows what is best for the country." Then he added proudly, "I guess if the President is that kind of a man, I shouldn't fuss about wearing rubbers."

E. Paul Hovey

22   THE CONSERVATIVE CRAB

Confess your faults one to another.   JAMES 5:16

There was once a crab that always kept to the old ways of doing things, and simply hated anything new. If anyone suggested that he should change his old habits in the slightest, he would become very upset indeed. He had two homes, this crab, one by the seaside—where he lived through the summer—and one a few miles inland—where he lived in the winter. Every spring he went from his country house to the seaside, and every autumn he traveled back to the country. And always he went along exactly the same path.

One spring he discovered that men had put up a telegraph pole right in the middle of his path! Oh, it made him very angry. His eyes popped out and he went quite red with fury.

"Does man think," he snarled, "that he will force me out of my usual path with this silly humming pole? Never! I have used this path all my life, and my fathers before me, and I'm not going to change now."

So the furious little fellow climbed the pole, paused on the top for a breather, and then climbed down the other side. "That will show them!" he said. But in a moment he found another pole, right in his path again! He was madder than ever now, but he climbed this one as he had the other. And behold, there stood another pole. Well, he was getting tired by this time, but he would not give in. So he climbed that pole too . . . and the next . . . and the next . . .

In the end he reached the sea, after climbing miles and miles of poles. It had taken him a long time, and he arrived very late in the season, a thin and worn-out shadow of himself. He didn't greatly enjoy what was left of his summer by the sea, for he was thinking all the time of his return journey. It did occur to him that perhaps he could walk round the poles; but no, he wouldn't change.

Autumn came, and he set out as usual, but not at all happy about it. He clambered up the first pole, wearily . . . wearily . . . till he reached the top. There he sat down to rest. It was awful to think of those miles and miles of poles. He couldn't go on with it. He couldn't even make himself climb down the pole. He just sat there, and sat there, till he died. What a stupid crab!

And yet there are people just like him. Many years ago in the land of Persia, there was a king called Darius. He was a good man, but in some ways rather stupid. He had appointed a number of men to help him rule. Most of them were Persians, but one of them, Daniel, was an Israelite. The others were

47

jealous of Daniel, both because the king liked him and because he was a foreigner. So they decided to get rid of him if they could.

First, they tried to find fault with the way he ruled, but they could find nothing wrong there. Then they noticed that he said his prayers every day to the God of Israel, and decided to catch him somehow over that. Full of cunning, they went to the king and asked him to make a law that if anyone prayed to anyone but the king during the next thirty days, he would be thrown into the den of lions.

Well, the king made the law to please them, and signed it with his royal seal. But, of course, Daniel took no notice of such a silly law, and prayed to God as usual. This was what his enemies wanted, and they hastened to tell the king that Daniel had broken the law. "Now," they said, "he must be thrown into the lions' den. For the laws of the Medes and the Persians cannot be altered."

The king was very upset, for he loved Daniel. He saw that he had made a very stupid law. But did he change it? Oh no. It wasn't the custom to change the law. So he let his friend go to the lions, rather than admit that he had been silly and try to put things right. Of course, God took care of Daniel, but that was no thanks to the king. Surely Darius was just as stupid as the crab that wouldn't change.

I hope you have more sense than that. If you make a mistake, it is far better to say, "I'm sorry. I made a mistake. I see what is right now and I'll try to do my best to put things right." You may be silly to make a mistake, but you'll be sillier if you go on making it, once you know it's wrong. Admit your mistakes, therefore, and ask for pardon if you have hurt someone by them, and then you can make a fresh start. Keeping on only makes matters worse.

"Confess your faults one to another," wrote James, "and pray one for another that ye may be healed." We're here to help one another to get over our faults, and we'll never do that so long as we won't admit them.

Ralph Byers

23   *TRYING TO ESCAPE FROM ONESELF*

And Peter . . . went out and wept bitterly.   MATTHEW 26:75

One summer I was terribly bothered by a large wasp. It had somehow got into the living room and was buzzing furiously near the large window which overlooks the lake. Three days previously I had been stung by a wasp, so I decided that this time I would get the wasp before it got me. But when I reached for the spray-gun, I found that there was no DDT left. However, I found a spray-tin of insect repellent which we normally sprayed on ourselves to protect us from flies while fishing. I squirted some of that on the wasp.

Then I saw a most curious sight. The wasp found himself covered with a substance which was most offensive to him. For five minutes or more he flew crazily up and down and across the window. He was trying to escape from himself. The insect repellent made him repulsive even to himself. But try as he would, he could not escape from himself. Finally, when he paused to gather strength for another burst of buzzing, I got him.

There are times in the life of each of us when we are overcome by guilt or shame. We know we have done wrong. We wish we could escape from ourselves. Peter felt that way in the story from which our text is taken. Three times he had denied the Lord whom he loved. When the realization of his disloyalty struck home, he was aghast at what he had done and he saw no way of putting it right.

Most human beings have similar experiences. Temptations often lead us into acts of disloyalty to our Lord and to our friends, and for a time we do not know how we can escape from the memory of what we have done. There is little to do but to go outside and weep bitterly.

But Peter did not allow his self-contempt and self-reproach to paralyze him for long. Having repented of his disloyalty and cowardice, he knew he could turn to Christ for forgiveness. When Christ forgave him, Peter found within himself the grace and strength to forget the past and to dedicate his future to the Lord. He had been a self-reproachful coward, but he became a staunch soldier of the faith. And Peter, when he had run his full course, no longer had reason to be ashamed of himself.

Walter C. Sellars

24   *A MAN WHO NEVER BECAME ANGRY*

Four hundred years before Jesus lived in Palestine there was a noble teacher in Athens by the name of Socrates. He was such a homely man that those who met him for the first time were never impressed by his appearance. He had a bald head and a turned-up nose. He wore baggy clothes and went barefoot in winter as well as in summer. Strangers who saw him walking about the streets of the city often mistook him for a beggar.

But he was so wise and good that he is considered one of the best men who ever lived.

His great purpose in life was to help young men acquire wisdom and teach them self-control. His method of teaching was not simply by talking to them and telling them what they ought to do, but by asking questions which helped them to discover their own faults and weaknesses, and gave them the desire to overcome them. He also knew that to be a good teacher he must set a good example. So he always followed the guidance of what we call conscience but he called the inner voice, which told him what was right and wrong.

One of the things which Socrates' inner voice told him was that he should never lose his temper and become angry. He never quarreled with anyone, not even his wife Xantippe, although she was said to have been a very disagreeable person to live with. She was always finding fault with him. One of the things she criticized him for, according to the stories that have been handed down to us, was because he did not take any pay for his teaching. Socrates didn't mind being poor. He thought people ought to do their work for the sake of helping others, and not to make money.

One day Xantippe scolded him more loudly than usual and Socrates left the house so that he would not have to listen to the sound of her angry voice. As he went out of the door, Xantippe seized a bucket of water and threw it over his head. Socrates was dripping wet but he didn't get mad. He said quietly, "After Xantippe thunders, rain may be expected."

Most people think it is a sign of weakness not to show their temper and make an angry reply if anyone does or says anything to them which is unkind. They consider it cowardly not to strike back if anyone hits them. They think they are showing their strength when they bluster and threaten. They imagine they are being brave when they act like a bully and challenge someone to a fight.

Socrates had different ideas. He believed that anger was a sign of weakness and that self-control was an indication of strength.

Like Jesus, Socrates was put to death by people who did not believe in his way of life and were jealous of his influence. Yet after nearly twenty-five hundred years people still reverence his memory because he was always true to the inner voice.

Walter Dudley Cavert

25   *STORY OF A QUARREL*

There is a story which says that two old hermits in the Egyptian desert lived happily together for many years. No quarrel ever disturbed their peace. In fact, when one of them spoke one day about quarreling, the other declared he didn't know what a quarrel was! "Well," said the first, "let us have a quarrel for a change, just to see what it is like." The other was a little doubtful, but being anxious to learn, he agreed to the experiment.

"This is how we'll do it," said his companion. "You see this stone? I'll put it here on the ground between us. When I say, 'This is mine,' you must say, 'No, it's mine.' Then I'll say in a louder voice, 'It isn't. I tell you it's mine.' In this way we will make a quarrel."

So they stood one on either side of the stone, and the first hermit began: "This is mine!" The second replied, "No, it's mine!" Then the first said in a very loud voice, "It isn't. I tell you it's mine!" "Very well, then," said the other, "if it's yours, by all means take it!"

They just couldn't go on quarreling after that, and so the quarrel ended before it had really begun. Don't you think it would be like that with most quarrels if only people were more kindly disposed to one another, anxious always, for their part, to live peaceably with all men?

H. W. Hitchcock

26   *THE CAMEL'S NOSE*

Thou shalt love the Lord thy God with all thy heart.   MATTHEW 22:37

The Arabs have a proverb, "Beware of the camel's nose." To understand what they mean by it, you must know this story. There was once a traveler riding his camel across the desert when a sudden storm blew up. He flung himself from his camel, quickly put up his little tent, wrapped some cloth over his mouth and nose to keep out the flying sand, and lay down to wait for it to blow itself out. By and by he heard the camel nuzzling at the fastenings of his tent.

"What do you want?" he demanded.

"Please, master," said the camel in a lowly voice, "may I share the shelter of your tent?"

"Don't be silly!" replied the traveler. "There is no room for us both in the tent."

"Well," said the camel, "at least let me get my nose in, so that I may breathe some clean air."

"Very well," said the traveler. "Your nose, and no more."

The camel pushed his nose inside. By and by the traveler felt a movement, and discovered that the camel's head and part of his neck were now inside.

"Get out!" he cried. "Didn't I say, 'your nose and no more'?"

"Yes, you did," admitted the camel. "But, after all, my neck isn't so very big, and there's plenty of room for it in here."

Well, the traveler didn't like it, but he said no more. By and by there was another movement, a strong one, and he was pushed against the side of the tent. He could hardly move, for now a large part of the camel's body was inside the tent. He would have liked to object, but found it hard to speak, and knew it would be no use anyway. The camel was stronger than he. He could never have put him out. Soon there was another movement which so squeezed him against the side of the tent that he was glad to slip underneath and escape. So in the end the camel was inside the tent and the traveler outside. That is why the Arabs say, "Beware of the camel's nose!"

It is really a warning against giving evil even the smallest place in our lives; for if we do, it soon demands more. There are wrong things that come to us and say, "Give me a little place in your heart. I'm only a little thing. I don't matter. What's a little lie, or a little theft, or a little unkindness? It won't make any difference, I promise you."

Maybe we let them in. By and by, we notice that there seems to be an increasing number of them. One lie leads to another. A theft has to be hidden by some other wrong thing. And one unkindness seems to bring others with it. Perhaps we decide that things are going too far, and now we will clear them all out—only to find that we cannot! Bad habits are hard to break.

We never meant them to grow so strong. We never meant them to take control. We meant to give our hearts to God, to whom they belong, and only to let in a little "camel's nose" of evil, but now—

Now do you see why Jesus, asked what was the chief commandment, replied, "You must love the Lord your God with all your heart"?*

Ralph Byers

27   *SISTER'S PIGGY BANK*

Thou God seest me.   GENESIS 16:13

Johnny had looked twice into every drawer in his room. Somewhere, he thought, there must be a quarter. He needed a quarter to buy a new ball or he would not be able to play with the other fellows. At last with a sigh he gave up. He couldn't even find a nickel in his room.

Suddenly he remembered his sister's piggy bank. It held lots of money. She saved her money wisely by dropping it into her little bank. "I saw her put some money in the piggy bank yesterday," Johnny said to himself. "If I shake the bank at least a quarter would come out. And she'd never know it was gone anyway."

Slowly and quietly Johnny went into his sister's room. Very carefully he shook the piggy bank. Several coins slipped out. He set the bank back on her dresser, but at that very moment he remembered the words of his last Sunday-school lesson. "Thou God seest me." The words rang in his ears repeatedly.

"If no one else sees me, God does," he thought. "I should not be doing this. When Christ was tempted, he did not fail. I should have asked him for strength to resist temptation." Then Johnny put the money back in the piggy bank.

As he turned to leave, a voice called to him. Johnny knew that it was his sister's voice. He was very ashamed of himself. Tremblingly he went toward his sister and looked into her kind, blue eyes. "Johnny," she said, "I was watching you just now. You had a tough fight, but you won. Here, take my hand. I'm proud of you."

Johnny was happy that he had such a wonderful sister. He knew she would forgive him. Then she said, "Tell me, Johnny, what you want and I'll help you to get it the right way."

J. Calvert Cariss

28   *A LITTLE THING CALLED SIN*

> Guard above all things, guard your inner self, for so you live and prosper. PROVERBS 4:23 (MOFFATT)

Once a kind old lady named Mrs. Brown lived in a neat little cottage beside a huge oak tree. How very much she admired that tall and beautiful tree. It had a massive trunk, great spreading branches, and green, lush leaves. During the summer when the sun was very warm it provided shade for her. During the autumn when the winds were blowing the tree was like a shelter for her house. Indeed, so wonderful was this oak tree that Mrs. Brown hoped it would bud and grow and live forever.

Mrs. Brown, however, was not aware that her oak tree was the center of a great argument. This heated discussion was on the question, "Who is the strongest: the rain, the wind, the snow, or the sun?"

Lady Rain said that she could prove her strength by pouring her heaviest showers down upon the big oak tree and thereby destroy it. Lord Wind, Princess Snow, and King Sun laughed at

Lady Rain. "Go ahead," they said. But after the shower, the tree was more healthy and greener than ever.

Then Lord Wind took his turn. He blew terrific gusts and gales across the hills and fields. The little cottage shook and creaked, but the tall oak tree was held fast by its roots. Not even a branch was broken.

Now Princess Snow had her turn. Her soft, white flakes fell upon the tree and at last not a leaf could be seen, for the tree was completely covered with snow. "You see," she said excitedly, "the tree is still now and it is dead."

"Let's find out," said King Sun. A great and brilliant smile crossed his face and the brightly shining rays warmed the whole earth. In a few minutes every snowflake was melted. And behold! the oak tree appeared more beautiful than before.

"Well, I give up," said King Sun. And the others agreed with him that they would use their strength to strengthen the tall oak tree.

Many months passed. Then on one spring day, when all the world was filled with the song of birds and the fragrance of blossoms, Mrs. Brown returned to her home after a trip to the South. She gasped in utter dismay and horror, for the great oak tree lay flat on the ground. What could have happened? Was it the wind, the rain, or the snow? Certainly not. Nor was it the sun. She immediately called in the woodcutters and they soon gave her the reason. When they sawed through the trunk, they found that the whole heart of the tree had been eaten away by thousands of tiny worms. The outside trunk looked healthy and strong, but the inside was destroyed.

Mrs. Brown examined the trunk very carefully and discovered one tiny hole where the first little worm had bored its way in.

Once inside, he multiplied into many, many thousands of other worms who had bored, gnawed, and chewed until the whole heart of the tree was gone.

The Bible says, "Guard above all things, guard your inner self, for so you live and prosper." That means that we must guard carefully what is inside of us, for it is the inside that really counts. If one little sin can get inside, it will multiply so quickly and easily into many other sins until your whole heart is wrong. No little boy or girl is strong until he or she is clean and good both on the inside and the outside.

Donald Macleod

29   *THE MAN ON HORSEBACK*

If any one would be first, he must be last of all and servant of all.
MARK 9:35 (RSV)

During the days of the Revolutionary War there was a tremendous need to build more and more forts. Ammunition had to be kept in safe places. People had to be protected. Battles had to be fought. Strong, safe shelters were needed.

On one occasion, while a group of men were busy building one of these forts, they struggled to put a particularly heavy log into place. The soldier, who was in charge of the workmen, called out: "Heave ho! Heave away, men!" The words were a chant to help the men pull together as they attempted to move the large log.

But the log wouldn't budge. Try as they might, the men could not get the log into place. Just as they were about to abandon their attempts, a man on horseback rode up. "Why don't you help them with the lifting?" he asked the soldier. "Don't you see that the log is heavy?"

The soldier answered: "I'm a corporal. I can't help with that kind of work."

The man on horseback dismounted and went over to the workmen. "Now," he said, "altogether, men. Heave ho! Heave ho!" And up went the log into its place. As the man went back to his horse, he said to the soldier, "Next time you have a heavy log to lift and you need help, just call for your Commander in Chief."

The man who said this was George Washington, the Commander in Chief. He was obeying the words of Jesus, "If any one would be first, he must be last of all and servant of all." Jesus meant that one of the best things we can do is to help someone else to lift a heavy load.

Donald Craig Kerr

4. THE IMPORTANCE OF LITTLE THINGS

❦

THE HORSESHOE NAIL

For who hath despised the day of small things? ZECHARIAH 4:10

One evening I was fishing a mile or more from camp. The casting reel was not working quite so smoothly as usual but I did not stop to examine it. Suddenly something dropped into the water and my fishing was over for that evening. A very small screw, so tiny I could scarcely find where it had been placed, had worked loose and fallen out; immediately the delicately made reel was useless. It was a very small object but it had an important part to play.

Then I realized what the old Mother Goose verse means:

> For want of a nail
>   The shoe was lost;
> For want of a shoe
>   The horse was lost;
> For want of a horse
>   The rider was lost;
> For want of a rider
>   The battle was lost;
> And all for the want
>   Of a horseshoe nail.

The Importance of Little Things

A young boy going downtown used to stop and watch a black smith at work. He enjoyed watching the sparks fly from the forge when the smithy pumped the bellows, and he liked to see the red-hot iron hammered into shape on the anvil. One thing he noticed particularly: the old blacksmith never seemed to be satisfied. He hammered and beat, then heated and hammered again on the same link of an enormous chain which he was making. Again and again, when it seemed to the boy that the link was perfect, the smithy would thrust it back into the fire, heat till red-hot, and begin all over again.

"Why do you do that so often; don't you ever tired of it?" asked the boy.

"Of course, I get tired, but I want this link to be welded correctly. If I don't do it perfectly, I may be taking someone's life," the blacksmith replied.

Of course, the boy did not understand, but the old smithy knew that some day there might be a storm at sea and then all his careful toil would not be for nothing.

After many months the chain was completed, and the captain of a sailing vessel came to claim it. Loading the enormous chain on the vessel, he sailed away to a distant port. Some months after, they were nearing home when a tempest swept down upon them. The vessel was being rapidly driven toward dangerous rocks; the crew could hear the breakers roar, and knew that the ship might soon be dashed to pieces. There was only one thing to do: throw out the anchors. One was thrown overboard but no sooner had it caught on a rock than a link parted and the vessel leaped ahead into the terrible darkness. Another anchor was thrown out with the same result.

Finally the captain shouted: "Throw out the last one! If this one breaks, we are lost!" They threw it. A few moments of awful suspense followed; then it caught for an instant, dragged free, and caught again. This time it held; the sturdy, strong chain did not part.

Why? Because an old blacksmith way back there in that shop knew the value of little things. That last small detail of perfection in welding the links did not seem important to the boy, but it was tremendously vital to the captain and his ship.

There are times when it does not seem necessary to boys and girls to be careful about details. "It isn't just right but I'll let it go. Just once won't matter," they say. But once does matter. The lack of a horseshoe nail lost a battle; the loss of a tiny screw ruined a reel; and just one weak link would have meant a wrecked ship.

If ever you are tempted to scorn small things, remember that life depends more upon the small than upon the large. A weak link in your character may allow your life to be thrown upon the rocks of failure.

Despise not the day of small things.

Carl S. Weist

31   *NOTHING*

Be careful for nothing.   PHILIPPIANS 4:6

There are a great many apparently simple words which are not easy to define. Take "nothing," for example; it isn't easy to say what nothing is, especially when you remember that nothing is something that is not. Of course, when you put it that way it just sounds silly. But could you define nothing? You needn't scratch your head as if you were beginning to think about it, for you never could do it. Perhaps a very wise philosopher could do it; he would make a great deal out of nothing, and after he had finished nobody would be any the wiser. That doesn't mean that you don't know what nothing is. You know that perfectly well, only it is difficult to explain. The trouble is that you don't always mean nothing when you say, "Nothing."

Maybe you've been rude to someone and your mother gets to know of it and asks, "What did you say to Mrs. So-and-so?" then you look angelically innocent and say, "Nothing." Or perhaps you've been misbehaving in some other way; you've nearly been caught but not quite, yet you have a guilty look and Father says, "What have you been up to?" and once again you reply, "Nothing." On such occasions you don't really mean "nothing," do you? Your "nothing" means something, so that your "nothing" is a lie.

Or again, at school this time, you have been inattentive. You haven't been putting your mind to your work; you've been thinking nothing. So when you try to do the new kind of problem in arithmetic, which the teacher has just been showing you how to do, you get it wrong, and round comes teacher and puts a big red or blue zero on your exercise book. You get nothing for a wrong solution to the problem. Here nothing really means ignorance, ignorance that is entirely your own fault and ignorance that leads you into error.

Then, too, when a chum has been telling you about something he has done, it may be a prize he has won, a place he has visited or just some good thing that has happened to him, you sometimes say, "Oh, that's nothing!" But you really don't mean that it is nothing, for it is something that you'd like to have happened to you. Nothing then means envy.

In these ways you often make nothing mean an awful lot of things which it doesn't usually mean and which, in fact, it does not really mean. You see, when you speak like that you are actually saying or acting as if you believed that such things as lying, ignorance and envy are nothing, and these are fearful things to think and believe. This is something about which you must be very careful. It isn't exactly this that the Apostle had in mind when he wrote to the members of the Church in Philippi saying, "Be careful for nothing," but you must be careful for nothing as you sometimes mean it.

Jesus himself said that people who thought nothing of certain things were foolish and blind. He was speaking of people who make vows and show their intention of keeping them by swearing their vows "by the temple" or "by the altar." To Jesus that sort of thing was a kind of blasphemy, something like taking God's name in vain. The people who did that sort of thing said, "It is nothing." Jesus said they were foolish and blind.

Lying, ignorance and envy, and all the other things of which you think nothing, can make you foolish and blind too. Foolish because thinking such things is harmful to you; and blind because they keep you from seeing the wrongness of them, because they shut your eyes to such things as truth and honesty, your need of learning and that unselfishness which keeps you from envy. You are taught to believe that Jesus is the Truth. How then can you believe that a lie is nothing? You know that Jesus is the Teacher sent from God. How then can you believe that ignorance is nothing? And Jesus is the Saviour of the world because he took no thought for himself. How then can you think that your envy means nothing? So if you would be true and wise and unselfish be careful of those things of which you so often think nothing.

J. B. Wilson

32   *THE ORDER OF NEAR ENOUGH*

Almost. ACTS 26:28

Are any of you children members of the O.N.E.? Do you know of such a society? It is a very old Order and goes back for centuries. Yet it is an Order which is to be avoided by all boys and girls who are out to do good work.

You know the story of the trial of St. Paul before Agrippa, and that when the Apostle had finished his defense, the judge said, "Almost . . ." Agrippa belonged to this society of O.N.E. He was almost persuaded to become a Christian, but he did not go as far as Paul desired him to go. Agrippa was not thorough enough to take the last step—he left the matter incomplete. You see again how he showed himself a member of this Order when he said, Paul might have been set at liberty "But!" In the Order of Near Enough, Agrippa must be regarded as a leading official.

There is another very prominent member of this Order in English history. Every boy and girl who has to learn about the kings of England knows about Ethelred the Unready. He was never quite prepared. It was near enough for him to buy off the Danes when they attacked him. If you begin to buy off people, then they come again and again, and the Danes kept coming until they took the kingdom from this never-ready king. He was a member of the O.N.E.

I read of a scientist who said that all his students ought to be decorated with this Order. They knew that in the mathematics they had to do accuracy was demanded, but they turned lazy or tired, and said, "Oh, this is near enough." As soon as they said that they were failures—they were inaccurate, they were not doing their best work. You know that when you are doing mathematics it is not good enough to say you are within a fraction of the right answer, when the right answer is within your power to reach.

O.N.E. is responsible for a great deal of the careless work done by boys and girls. Membership in such a society is fatal to the best endeavors.

You remember that when Jesus was nearing the end of his life he said, "I have finished the work which thou gavest me to do" (John 17:4).

The Apostle Paul said, "I press toward the mark" (Phil. 3:14). He had an ideal and was moving towards it. And you know it is said that he wrote to Timothy and said to the young man, "I have fought a good fight, I have finished my course, I have kept the faith" (2 Tim. 4:7). He was not content to nearly finish—he had finished the course.

There are some Orders I should very much like to see all the boys and girls join, but I hope you will all keep clear of the O.N.E. Life is too important to put anything into it less than the best.*

T. Greener Gardner

33 *SOMETHING FOR NOTHING*

Every man's work shall be made manifest. 1 CORINTHIANS 3:13

Many, many times man's judgment is wrong. Only God's judgment is always right. Sometimes it happens that a man must wait for years to have his work properly judged.

More than eighty years ago there died a man who was always poor. Yet after his death one thing he had painted sold for $160,000. It is a picture called *The Angelus*. The artist was a Frenchman by the name of Millet. He sold the painting for a few hundred francs in French money.

He was born of poor and humble parents. He had to work on the farm. A clergyman taught him to read Latin. Young Millet began to read the Bible. In the Bible he had were a number of pictures. The boy began to copy these and that was the beginning of his lessons in art. His first teacher was the Bible.

He later studied with several artists. For a time he was in the city of Paris. But always he was poor. He had an ideal in art. His ideal meant more to him than money.

Sixteen years before he died he was still fighting poverty. Besides that he was fighting sickness in his home. He had painted many fine works of art which have later sold for large sums. But never did he receive much for this work. Fighting poverty and sickness he needed money to live. He managed to get together what in our money would be the sum of 75 cents. With this he bought some paint and brushes. He used a piece of canvas he had. He could not afford models. So he had developed a fine memory. He would watch people, remember what he wanted, and later transfer this to canvas. A peasant scene had impressed him. The people were poor like himself. With the brushes and paint he had bought he put it on canvas. The result was that beautiful painting, *The Angelus*. And he sold it for a few hundred francs.

The Angelus is the ringing of the Roman Catholic church bells at certain times of the day. These bells call the people to prayer. I once lived in a small town where the Angelus was rung. At the sound of the bells the people would stop what they were doing and bow their heads in prayer. Millet had often seen the poor farmers in the fields put down their tools and bow in prayer. That is what he put on canvas. There we see the simple reverence for God. It is a deeply religious painting and has inspired thousands.

Now and then we hear people talking about getting something for nothing. Since Millet spent what would have been 75 cents in our money for material, I suppose they would say his painting was something for nothing. But was it? Back of it was inspiration, prayer, ability and work. No, one never gets something for nothing.

Back of this painting was also the quest of an ideal. Millet might have worked for mere money. Had he done so he would have been numbered with thousands whose names are unknown. He toiled for something more than money. In that reaching for an ideal he left a priceless treasure for all men. There are things in life which money cannot buy.

Remember, you will get nowhere if you are always looking for something for nothing. You must give yourself to a high and noble calling. You must seek after the ideal. And there is no higher ideal than that which Jesus holds before you.

W. R. Siegart

5. THE VOICE OF CONSCIENCE

❦

THE ENGINE-ROOM TELEGRAPH

How many of you have read *Tom Sawyer?* If you haven't read it, you should, for it's lots of fun from beginning to end. If you have read it, do you remember a character named Ben Rogers? Maybe I can help you recall him. When Tom Sawyer saw him, he wasn't Ben Rogers at all. Do you know why? He was a river-steamer. Imagine! He was the *Big Missouri*, and he was drawing nine feet of water. Then, suddenly, Ben Rogers ceased to be a boat and became its captain shouting commands: "Set her back on the starboard." Do you think that satisfied him? No. In a split second he changed from being the skipper to become the bells in the engine room singing out, "Ting-a-ling-ling." But Tom Sawyer paid no attention. He continued to whitewash the fence until, for an apple core, he allowed Ben to become an outdoor artist.

Tom Sawyer makes me think of my boyhood in Scotland and of a lovely body of water in southwest Scotland called the Firth of Clyde. On those waters were perky little steamers which stopped at one pier after another. Like Ben Rogers, we used to play at being these boats, and their captains, and their bells, and their paddle wheels. We borrowed the clothesline and for hours we would throw the rope to our small brothers and sisters who were the pier masters. We played in Scotland the same games Tom Sawyer and his gang played on the Mississippi River.

Sometimes during the summer we would sail on these Clyde steamers. The most thrilling part of that event was to go down below and watch and listen to the engines, huge masses of shining steel which turned the paddles or twisted the propellers. We watched the engineer while he kept track of the engine-room telegraph. It had a large face with a pointer on it. On this face were words reading, "Ahead: Full, Half, Slow, Stand By" and "Astern: Full, Half, Slow, Finished With Engines." Between these was the word "Stop" in red letters. The engineer moved the levers whenever the captain signaled his command on the telegraph. He never argued or debated. He just obeyed. He did what the telegraph told him that the captain wanted done.

We are like the engineers on the Clyde steamers and on the Mississippi River boats. There is a captain on the bridge. He is God. He is in charge. Sometimes he turns over his power and responsibility to our parents. They are his officers and they, too, must be obeyed. All orders come from the person on the bridge. Within each of us is an engine-room telegraph. It is called "conscience." Through our conscience, God lets us know what he expects us to do: "Full Speed Ahead," "Stop," or "Stand By For Orders."

Why does God speak to us through our conscience? Because we are the engineers. We move the levers which start and stop the engines. Sometimes we do not obey the telegraph. It rings out "Stop," and we go ahead and say what we know we shouldn't say. It orders "Full Speed," but we would rather stop, for we don't really want to do God's bidding. It signals "Astern," because there is trouble ahead. But we keep on going and then there is a crash. But when we do obey, we are surprised and pleased by the smooth sailing.

God is our captain and he gives the orders. Conscience is our telegraph and it signals to us what God wants us to do. We are the engineers and we are supposed to obey.

In the evening, when the telegraph says "Finished With Engines," let each of us have a talk with the Captain. We can do that by reading the Bible and by saying our prayers to him. And in the morning we shall be in good shape when the telegraph rings "Stand By" and we make ready for another day of voyaging.

James T. Cleland

35   *LIE DETECTOR*

> But a certain man named Ananias, with Sapphira his wife, sold a possession, and kept back part of the price, his wife also being privy to it, and brought a certain part, and laid it at the apostles' feet.
> ACTS 5:1-2

This happened way back there at the beginning of the Christian Church. The Christians were so much "of one heart and soul" that they had all their possessions in common and no one said that he or she owned anything. When one of them sold a piece of land or a yoke of oxen, he would bring in all the money and put it in the common bank. The apostles then would give to the members of the colony according to their needs.

This is where Ananias and Sapphira step into the picture. Ananias sold some land but he did not bring in all of the price. He figured that he would continue to live from the common fund, and at the same time have a little extra on hand which he could use for his wife and himself in any way they wished.

Today we would call it hoarding. It was not honest, of course, and it did not work.

"Why did you keep back part of the price, Ananias?" asked Peter. "You have not lied unto men, but unto God." When Ananias heard these words, the shock was too great and he fell down dead. Sapphira, his wife, was then called in, and when Peter asked why they had agreed together to lie about the price, she too fell down dead, and was carried out.

Were Peter living today he might have used what is called a "lie detector." It is an instrument used by the police when a person accused of a crime is being questioned. The sensitive machine registers the tenseness or nervous state of the one under suspicion. It does not always work, but very often they can tell by it when the accused person answers whether he is telling the truth. The pressure of nervousness rises very high when a question is put which might involve the prisoner in a crime. If the accused answers very calmly while the detector reveals a high degree of excitement underneath, the police figure that the man is lying.

But Peter had a better instrument; we may call is a "truth detector." He simply faced Ananias and Sapphira with the facts and let conscience do the detecting. Conscience—what kind of an apparatus is that, do you ask? Well, conscience is something in our hearts which tells us at once whether a thought and deed are right or wrong. It is a kind of voice which whispers very quietly, "You should do this," or "You shouldn't do that," "It would not be kind; it is not honest."

No lie detector ever invented could be as sensitive as this truth detector which every one of us possesses. If any of you have ever tried cheating in an examination, or not telling your parents the whole truth about what happened yesterday, you will remember that you did not feel exactly right. You moped about, out of sorts with everything and especially with yourselves. The trouble was of course that the truth detector was working, and somehow you knew that you were lying not simply to teacher or parents but to God.

For conscience is the voice of God. God has placed this sense of right and wrong deep within us, and when we disregard conscience, we are in a way disregarding God.

How important then that we listen to this voice, for if we do not listen, after a while our hearing may be dulled and we lose our delicate sensitiveness to right and wrong, which is the worst calamity that can come to us. So, let your conscience be your guide; but keep that conscience sharp and clear that it may be to you always as a bright light in a dark night.

Carl S. Weist

36   *A TROUBLED CONSCIENCE*

A good conscience. 1 TIMOTHY 1:19

Let me tell you a detective story. Once there was a great Indian prince who found that someone had stolen from his treasure house in the night. He called all his wise men together, and asked them to find the thief. One of the wise men said: "I can do what you want. At home I have some magic sticks. And this is their magic. When any of them is in the company of a thief, it grows. It will shoot up as much as two inches in a single night. If your majesty will have all your servants shut up tonight in separate cells, we shall put a stick in each cell, and, in the morning, your majesty will find that one of the sticks has grown two inches. Then we shall know the guilty man." So this was done.

Next morning the sticks were gathered and measured. It was found that one of them was two inches *shorter* than the others. The king thought that the magic had gone wrong. Then the wise man explained. That was just what he expected to happen. He pointed to the man who had handed in the short stick, and said, "Your majesty will find that this man is the thief." The man at once confessed. "I knew," he said, "that if any of the sticks grew longer than the others, it would be mine. And no one can imagine the agony I went through last night. Every few minutes I looked at the stick to see whether it was giving me away. At last I began to imagine that it was growing. Then I felt certain. It was half an inch longer. Then it was an inch. By early morning it was two inches longer. So I cut off two inches to make it the same as the others." That was just what the wise man had expected to happen. There was nothing magic in the sticks, but he knew how conscience would work, and so he had caught the guilty man.

Keep a good conscience. Then nothing can make you afraid. That man had a bad conscience. But there is a worse conscience even than that. A little Indian boy once told what it is like. "It is a little three-cornered, sharp thing in here," he said, pointing to his heart. "And when I do wrong it turns round and round and hurts very much. But if I keep on doing wrong, it will turn and turn, till all the sharp edges are worn away, and then it won't hurt any more."

That is the worst kind of conscience—one that doesn't hurt any more. We have killed it. Perhaps we have told a lie, and conscience hurts terribly. If we go on telling lies, it doesn't hurt so much, till, finally, it stops hurting altogether. We have bound and gagged it. And when we are walking into danger, it cannot even cry out "Stop!"

Keep a good conscience, a conscience in good repair.*

Edgar Primrose Dickie

37   *THE CLOCK WITHOUT HANDS*

A friend of mine showed me the other day a beautiful old clock of which he was very proud. He told me its history, how his great-grandfather had gone to bed by it and got up by it for seventy-five years, and how his own father had had it for seventy-five years more. He said he himself had got off to school by it when he was a boy, and that many of his boyhood memories were associated with this old clock. He also told me what a wonderful time-keeper the clock was. It was very accurate and very dependable.

But there was one thing I noticed about the clock when I saw it: it had no hands. I have no doubt that my friend was telling the truth when he said it was a good time-keeper and that the works were in perfect condition. But the clock wasn't telling time when I saw it. He set the works going, and they went. I could hear the regular tick-tock, tick-tock, tick-tock, but the face of the clock said nothing, because the hands were off.

As I came away I said, "How like some boys and girls that old clock is! They may be good on the inside and mean all right, but you'd never know it by the way they act. They are like the clock without hands."

There is a verse in the Bible that says: "If ye *know* these things, happy are ye if ye *do* them" (John 13:17). It isn't enough to know what is right, and to feel like doing what is right. You must do it, or people won't know anything about all your good thoughts and feelings. You will be like the clock without hands.

Then there are other boys and girls who resemble that old clock in another way. The old clock went right on talking, with its tick-tock, tick-tock, just as if it were telling time. It sounded like a real time-teller. But its face told nothing. There are some boys and girls who talk big about what fine things they're going to do, but they never do them. They are about as useful as the old clock for the real business of life.

Jesus told about a boy who was quite like them. His father said to him one morning, "Son, go work today in my vineyard." And he said, "I go, sir," and he went not (Matt. 21:28-30). Big talk, you see, but nothing done. A clock without hands. Ralph Waldo Emerson once said: "What you *are* speaks so loudly I can't hear what you *say*."

About the only way people are going to know that you are all right on the inside is by your actions. It's no use, for instance, for you to tell your mother you love her, and then go and do something she has told you not to do. Your actions speak louder than your words. You say you are "good at heart." All right, people are waiting to be shown. They won't take you for what you *say* you are. You are a clock without hands until you *do* the right thing.

Howard J. Chidley

38 *HANDSOME IS AS HANDSOME DOES*

Scripture: LUKE 6: 43-49

A very small boy came home crying one day, and when his mother asked him what was the matter, he said, "I caught a pretty fly, and it bit me." So, his mother explained that it must have been a bee or a wasp. And some bees and some wasps are very beautiful; but they can sting terribly.

Well, he was a very small boy, as I said; but he learned a very big lesson. That lesson is that we mustn't judge things by the way they look.

An acorn has a smooth, pretty shell, but the meat in it is bitter; and a Brazil nut has a rough, hard, irregular shell, but, O, how sweet the meat is.

The other day I went by a five-and-ten-cent store, and although it was a warm day, there was a window filled with cups of delicious-looking ice cream and great, tall glasses of ice cream sodas, topped with whipped cream and a red, ripe cherry, and even a straw. Well, since the sun was shining right on them, I waited a few moments to see them melt; but they didn't. It was imitation ice cream and imitation soda!

Once I was riding on a street car, and a beautifully dressed girl got on just behind a dear old lady; and when I looked at the girl, I said to myself, "What a very nice young lady that is," but—unfortunately—she pushed by the dear old lady and grabbed the only seat left in the car, and the old lady had to stand until I gave her my seat.

You see, children, being a lady or a gentleman means having something in the heart, much more than the kind of clothes we wear. So, we can't judge entirely by appearances.

When I was a little boy, my mother was always saying to me, "Handsome is as handsome does," and that's a good thing to remember.

So, while all of you look like very nice, polite, well-reared children, I do hope that is the kind of children you really are.

It is what we are inside that counts; and the only way in which we can show what we are in our hearts is by our behavior. That is why our mothers and fathers try so hard to teach us good manners—because even if we are fine persons, but don't know how to behave ourselves before others, we shall be misjudged, and—not only that—but our fathers and mothers, too!

So, all of us are responsible not only for our own reputations but for the reputations of our parents, too; and my mother was right when she taught me, "Handsome is as handsome does."

Raimundo de Ovies

39   *PAINTERS OF SUNSETS*

A sunset won't wait for you to paint it. Even while you are watching and getting your paints out of the box, the orange in the sky changes to red, and the blue to purple. And all the clouds you wanted for the top of the picture blow away into New Jersey or North Carolina, or go to bed.

When a person draws a picture of a wooden box, he knows the box will stand there just as long as he wants it to. He can go home to dinner, or take a walk, or come back the next day; and, sure enough, when he comes back it will be just the way it was.

It's the same way with a dog. If the dog won't stand still when you're trying to draw his picture you can always lead him back to where he was before and try again. If you coax him enough he will point his ears up just the way they were, and put the left paw in front of the right paw.

But a sunset won't wait! When it's gone, it's gone; and you can't coax it to come back. You can say to it: "Wait just a minute. Hold it. Stay where you are. I want to get my paintbox." But it won't hear you. Like the weather, it never changes its plans no matter what people say. When you come back with your paints and brushes, you can paint instead a picture of the moon coming up, or the lights in the houses being turned on; but you won't be able to paint the sunset.

"Well, there'll always be another one tomorrow," you say. Of course there will be. But it won't be quite the same—with a long streak of orange just here and a patch of pale blue just there. The sun has gone down nearly every night since your grandfather was a boy, and maybe a year or two before that, but there have never been two sunsets exactly alike since the world began—just as there have never been two babies exactly alike, or two kittens.

So, if you like to paint, and if you want a sunset for your picture, you must learn to work fast, with brushes in both hands and one eye on the clock. It must all be finished in half an hour.

Now, when you're painting a sunset, and there's a fence or a barn or a pile of stones nearby, and you try to put them in, that means you won't have so much time for the sunset itself, doesn't it? If you have thirty minutes all together, and if you spend twenty minutes on the fence posts and the barn, you'll have only ten minutes left for the sky. When you have finished and take the picture home, you may have a rather pretty barn, but your sunset won't amount to much.

There aren't only a thousand painters of pictures in the world, boys and girls. All of us are painters. And because we're Christian people, we're all painting sunsets—or trying to. And sometimes we're so busy with small thoughts and small things that really don't matter, like old fences and red barns, that we haven't time to paint all the glory that fills the west when the sun is setting.

There isn't time to paint both. It is up to us to *choose* which we want in our picture. The fence is nice, and so is the barn; but I think I'll paint a deep blue heaven with a great golden sun going down in the west. In my picture I've been thinking I'll paint a sunset! What are *you* going to paint?*

Wayne A. Nicholas

40   *SIGNATURE TUNE*

Tom stood outside his friend's house whistling. He kept repeating the first few bars of a popular tune. A gentleman passing at the time asked, "Is that all you know of the tune?"

"No. I know it all through," Tom replied.

"Then why not whistle it all instead of stopping after the first few bars?"

"Oh," was the reply, "because it is my signature tune."

"Your signature tune?" inquired the man. "Whatever do you mean?"

"You know what a signature tune is," was the reply. "All the bands and organists on the radio have one. It is a piece of music they play at the commencement of their broadcast; then listeners know whose band is playing."

"I see," replied the man. "And who is listening to you?"

Pointing to a nearby house, Tom replied, "I am whistling to my friend. He lives there, and when he hears the two lines of 'Swanee River' he knows that I am here. Then he comes out, and off we go to play."

The gentleman went on his way, while Tom whistled again the opening bars of his signature tune. As he went along he was thinking, "That boy's signature tune is something by which he is known." He liked Tom's tune, it was cheerful; but then Tom looked a cheerful kind of boy. "I wonder what my signature tune is?" This thought ran through his mind, and others, "What am I known by? Something sad or cheerful, good or bad?"

How many children know what their signature tune is? If someone says, "I know a little boy who is always grumbling," does the listener immediately think of you? When someone thoughtful and jolly is mentioned, are you thought of immediately? It is said that when some visitors went to a certain mission field they spoke of the love and kindness of their Master. The natives immediately thought of their missionary friend, and replied, "Yes. We know him; he lives amongst us." What a lovely signature tune!

You will remember how Goliath came and roared out his challenge to the Israelites, night and morning: "Why are ye come out to set your battle in array? am not I a Philistine, and ye servants to Saul? choose you a man for you, and let him come down to me. If he be able to fight with me, and to kill me, then will we be your servants: but if I prevail against him, then shall ye be our servants, and serve us. . . . I defy the armies of Israel this day; give me a man, that we may fight together" (I Sam. 17:8-10). This was his signature tune. "He came out and spake according to the same words."

Everyone has a signature tune; it is our reputation. It is made up of the kind of things we say and do. It is a wise thing, but not an easy one, to ask someone what they think your signature tune is. Ask them what they think of it! If it is nasty, cruel or boastful, change it. Take care to choose in its place something which reminds people of Jesus Christ.

Douglas A. Smith

41 *CONTRARY WINDS*

The wind was against them. MARK 6:48

These words tell of a difficulty which the disciples had on the Sea of Galilee. The strong winds were blowing against them, and they feared that they might never reach land again. You and I know how they felt, for often our efforts seem to be stopped by the strong winds of discouragement and doubt.

When I was a boy I learned that the strong wind can be helpful. An expert kite-maker told me how to make and fly many kinds of kites. One of the first lessons I learned I have always remembered. Being inexperienced, I tried to fly my first kite by taking a firm hold on the string and then running as fast as I could in the same direction as the wind was blowing. Well, you know what happened. The kite just dragged along on the ground and was soon broken.

Then my friend the kite-maker helped me to make a better kite and before I tried to launch this one he hinted that this time I should run in the opposite direction. It seemed strange to me that a kite should need a contrary wind to lift it off the earth. But I followed my friend's advice and ran sturdily into the wind. Immediately the kite rose from my hand and, when it got over the housetops and found a steady wind, I stopped running and my kite continued to rise as long as I unwound more twine from the ball in my hand. High in the air it floated, moving gracefully from side to side with the gentle cross-currents. It reached a great height on the very wind which blew against it.

Years later I joined the air force and I learned that an airplane, too, will rise only by facing the wind and racing down the runway until the very wind which blew against it lifted it safely into the air.

Some boys and girls never learn to deal with contrary winds. They are quite content as long as the wind is behind them, helping them along in the direction they have chosen. But they give up easily when troubles oppose them. These young people never make the most of their lives and of the opportunities God gives them. They are soon outdistanced by the ones who have learned to press on with courage and determination even when they have to confront a contrary gale.

Boys and girls who rise to the greatest heights of living are those who have learned the secret of the kite and the airplane. They climb above the uncertain gusts of discouragement and disappointment on the very wind which blows against them.

Walter C. Sellars

42   *MIND THE LIGHT*

The wind howled around the eaves of the little room where William Starr lay in his four-post bed, staring into the dark. A bare branch squeaked against the roof and the window-panes rattled furiously. William hardly heard them, although without thinking he pulled the thick quilt closer around his shoulders. The moaning and whistling of the most piercing gales were usually music to his ears, lulling him in his warm bed to a deeper and more delicious sleep. Now sleep was far away. He heard only one sound—and that not in his ears, but speaking to his heart.

"William Starr," it seemed to say, "rise out of thy bed and carry my message to the people of Clearbrook."

So strangely vivid the command came that he almost answered aloud, forming the words with his lips in the darkness.

"To Clearbrook, Lord? Surely thou canst not mean that I shall ride on this wild night those forty miles. I have received no summons from there to come."

"Thy summons comes from me. Ride thou to Clearbrook before the dawn."

"Oh, Lord, what message shall I deliver for thee there?" William almost groaned.

"Ride thou to Clearbrook," the Voice replied.

It was not strange to William to hear the Voice of God speaking to him clearly out of the darkness, and it was his simple habit to obey. On such a wild night as this, however, his body almost rebelled. He lay for several minutes fighting with himself. Then with a bound, he threw back the soft warm covers and stood barefooted in the numbing draft. Forty miles to Clearbrook— eight hour's hard riding through partly frozen mud. At least half the distance must be covered before dawn, and he did not know what message he was to give. Blindly, he dragged on his clothes, stumbled to the barn, and finally rode off into the night, urging his unwilling horse toward Clearbrook.

At ten o'clock next morning the people of the little village of Clearbrook were gathered in their meetinghouse. The company had been deep in silent worship for several minutes when a horse was heard galloping up to the door. A few turned their heads as a tall, weary-looking, mud-spattered man strode up the aisle and took a seat in the gallery. All were filled with curiosity. After the silence had continued unbroken for some time, William Starr rose stiffly and stood before them. Still, the message he was to deliver to these people had not been given to him, still he waited for further words of God. The Voice was silent.

Slowly and with much embarrassment he told of the command which had come to him in the night. "I have obeyed, I have ridden to deliver the message to you—and—the message goes no further." He sat down, his face flushed, his eyes troubled.

The people sat as awestruck as though a miracle had been performed before their eyes. They knew well the fearful roads over which William Starr had traveled; they thought of the bitter hours of darkness and of the wind that still raged. They thought of the times without number when they, too, had heard the Voice of God in their hearts, and had not heeded it.

Finally, an old man rose and said, solemnly, what all were thinking, "Indeed, our friend has delivered his message. It is, 'Mind the Light.' "

The Children's Story Garden

43   LETTERS FROM GOD

"Why cannot we see God?" one of my little friends asked. "If God is real, why cannot we see him?" Every one of you boys and girls has asked that question.

My friend's question is similar to another, "Why cannot we see an atom?" No one has ever seen an atom. Even the most powerful microscope fails in this respect. But we all believe in atoms. We have seen the picture of the submarine *Nautilus*, which is now operating in the deep seas through atomic power. Soon there will be trains and planes and ships driven by the power released from atoms. Electricity is now being released through huge atomic power plants. If no one has ever seen an atom, if we cannot know one by sight, or smell, or hearing, or feeling, how, then, do we know about atoms? Because we have seen atoms working. In the same way we know about electricity, or the magnetic force we call gravitation, or love. No one has ever seen electricity, or magnetic force, or love; but all of us have seen the results. The same is grandly true about God. Listen to these beautiful words of the Nineteenth Psalm:

> The heavens are telling the glory of God;
> And the firmament proclaims his handiwork.
> Day to day pours forth speech,
> And night to night declares knowledge. . . .
> Their voice goes out through all the earth,
> And their words to the end of the world.

The great Amrican poet, Walt Whitman, wrote, "In the faces of men and women I see God. I find letters from God dropped in the street and everyone is signed by God's name."

No, we have not seen God, but we have letters from God dropped in the street, in our own homes, on the mountains and in the forests and skies. There is a beautiful letter from God in every sunset, in the fragrance of a flower, the song of a lark, in the harmony of great music! We cannot see God with our eyes, but we have his letter to us in the majestic glory of the universe with its orderly procession of planets and stars and suns, and the equally orderly and amazing universe within the atom. One of the great scientists put it, "We think God's thoughts after him."

The most valued of all God's letters to us is the one dropped in a manger in Bethlehem on that first Christmas so many years ago. The letter written in the life and love of Jesus, in his teachings and influence, in his victory over evil and death, has been read by countless millions of people during the last two thousand years. Their lives have been changed from defeat to conquest, from sorrow to joy, from despair to confidence. For in the

life of Jesus we have seen most clearly what God is like. Since
God is like Jesus, we know he is interested in each of us. He will
forgive us when we have done wrong and will help us to do
right. He will lead us into paths of happy service for others so
that our lives may also become letters from God.

This is a beautiful thought, isn't it? You and I, in our words
and acts, even in our faces, may be letters from God, signed by
his name! That means that our friends and our loved ones, and
even strangers who happen to meet us, may see in us that which
helps them to believe in the goodness and love of God. But this
is true only when our attitudes and acts are like the spirit of
Jesus. If they represent the spirit of selfishness, or spite, or unkindness, or thoughtlessness, the letter is lost and God's love is
unknown.

Where is God?

> "O where is the sea?" the fishes cried,
> As they swam the crystal clearness through;
> "We've heard from of old of the ocean's tide,
> And we long to look on the water's blue.
> The wise ones speak of the infinite sea,
> Oh, who can tell us if such there be?"

Like the fish swimming in the sea and yet unable to see the sea,
or the lark in the sky who is unable to see the air, so we on earth
are surrounded, blessed, helped by God, though we are unable
to see him. But we have letters from God, dropped everywhere
in our universe and signed by his name. Let us pick up these
letters and read them so that our lives may reflect the goodness
and greatness of God.

Lance Webb

6. HELPING HANDS

❧

ANDREW AND THE BOY

> One of the two which heard John speak, and followed him was
> Andrew. . . . He first findeth his own brother Simon . . . and he
> brought him to Jesus.   JOHN 1:40-42

Andrew was a fisherman who knew and loved Jesus. He was
a good man who always was eager to meet and to know good
men. When he learned that a prophet by the name of John the
Baptist was preaching to great crowds of people, he followed
after the strange new prophet. It was in that way that he came
to know the Lord Jesus.

The first time Andrew ever saw Jesus was the day that John
baptized Jesus in the Jordan River. After that Andrew introduced his brother Simon Peter to the Master. At another time
some men from the land of the Greeks came to Andrew and
asked that he might take them to Jesus. Andrew led them to the
Master.

Andrew is mentioned in the Gospels for one thing, and that
was that he led people to Jesus. Unlike other disciples, Andrew
never healed a sick man and he never preached a great sermon.
He just led people to Jesus.

One day a great crowd of many thousands of people had
gathered to hear Jesus preach and teach. They listened for many
hours to his wonderful words. But they grew hungry, for at last
the sun was low in the west and they were in a country place.

Jesus asked Philip, one of the disciples who was near, "Where can we buy bread for this poor, weary crowd?" But Philip answered, "Why, Master, we have nothing for them." All of the disciples wondered how they might feed such a multitude. They were sorry for the fathers and mothers and especially for their small children. The little ones had looked and listened long to the man with the kindly eyes and loving smile. But now they were tired and hungry. Their cries rose above the hushed voices of mothers who tried in vain to quiet them. The disciples moved about restlessly, now rubbing their hands together, now shading their eyes, vainly hoping to catch sight of food vendors who might be somewhere at the edge of the great crowd. What should they do?

Almost unbelievingly, Andrew, who had sharper eyes than the rest, drew in his breath. He spotted a small boy who was carrying a lunch basket. Andrew hurried to the boy. Dodging this way and that way through the moving crowd, he at last reached the boy.

"Son," he said, "what have you there?"

The boy looked up quickly and answered, "Oh, my lunch. Mother insisted that I bring it along."

Overjoyed, the kindly big fisherman urged the boy along up the hill until they reached the Master.

"Here, Master, is food, five barley loaves and two small fish. It is not much, but it is something."

Looking down into the boy's upturned face, Jesus asked him if he would wish to share what he had with the other people. "Oh, yes, gladly," the boy responded. The boy was thrilled that he had been asked this by the man with the kind and gentle voice.

But the little boy did not lose his lunch. By giving so un-
selfishly of what he had, both he and the multitude had more
to eat than they needed. Jesus asked his disciples to quiet the
crowd by having them sit down on the thick grass which covered
the hillside. Then he thanked God and blessed the boy's food.
God caused it to multiply so that the disciples had enough food
for all of the eager people. They ate until they were satisfied,
and there was food left over.

Those people on the hillside that day were indeed thankful
to Jesus, but they ought also to have thanked God for the fisherman named Andrew who had led the little boy to the Master.
Andrew may not have done many spectacular things, but he did
lead people to Jesus.

Harold and *Alta Mason*

45   *SOMETHING FOR THE FELLOW
COMING AFTER*

Remembrance of . . . those that shall come after. ECCLESIASTES 1:11

There is an interesting story of the comradeship of men and
women in the old pioneering days in North America. It tells
how those people, settling in a new land to begin a new life,
helped one another. You know how, in their covered wagons,
they trekked over the prairies through the Indian country and
the buffalo lands to the golden west; you know because you've
read exciting stories or seen thrilling films of their adventures.
But do you know how they helped one another on the way?

Picture to yourself a family setting out for the west. As well
as provisions they had to take with them everything needed to
furnish a home—that log cabin which they intended to build

as soon as they found a suitable tract of country in which to settle. You can realize how the covered wagon must be very strongly built to carry such a heavy load. A long journey has to be made over difficult ground where there are swamps, loose sand, great heavy boulders and no roads. Think, too, of the horses or the oxen which have to pull the wagon. They have to be stong and in good condition, for the success of the expedition depends upon them. But even the best conditioned and strongest animals sometimes foundered on the way. Sometimes it was through lack of water or grazing, sometimes it was through the sheer exhaustion of pulling the heavy load over difficult country. If one animal foundered it meant that an extra strain was put upon those that remained. Had that been done the chances are that the expedition would have failed altogether. The only thing that could be done was to lighten the load. Foodstuffs were too precious to be dumped in this way, so it had to be some of the furniture and furnishings intended for the new home. This was done, and the discarded items were piled up by the side of the trail. But the man who was unfortunate enough to have to leave these things behind stuck a notice in the ground which read, "Take what you need but leave something for the fellow coming after."

As you journey through life have you ever thought that this is something which you all can do? You, too, can leave behind you something that can be shared by those who come after. You will agree that it certainly is a great thing to be able to do. But, perhaps, you are saying to yourselves, "What can we leave behind?" You mustn't think, however, that goods and chattels are the only things which can be left behind. A man once wrote these words, "I expect to pass through this world but once. Any good, therefore, that I can do, or any kindness that I can show to any fellow creature, let me do it now. Let me not defer or neglect it, for I shall not pass this way again."

Whoever the man was, he did think of leaving behind him a pleasant memory of one who was kind and good; who, long after he had passed on, would be remembered as one who helped his fellow men, a man who was a brother and a neighbour to all people in their needs. But not only that, he would leave behind him an example which could be followed by those who came after him, encouraging them to live as he did. You, too, can do that knowing that this is the Christian way. Of course, the supreme Example means us to go when he says, "Love one another, as I have loved you" (John 15:12). It is what the great apostle Paul had in mind when he said, "Bear ye one another's burdens, and so fulfil the law of Christ" (Gal. 6:2). You cannot do anything better with your life than just this and, in this way, to make things easier for the fellow coming after.*

J. B. Wilson

46 *SHORT ROPES*

I stood, the other day, watching a small boy with a rope in his hand about eight feet long, trying rather impatiently to hitch two doorknobs together which were at least nine feet apart. First he would shorten up the hitching end and then he would try to stretch the rope. Suddenly he dropped the rope and went out to the garage and came in with another piece. This he also tried, but it seemed to be even shorter than the first rope. When he was sure that this second rope would not reach, he just sat down and began to whimper a little. Then suddenly the sun came out for him and a bright idea solved the problem. He just took those two ropes and tied them together. Of course.

When I was a boy if some house or barn should catch on fire, every man and boy in the township would rush as fast as possible to help put it out. Each man would bring a pail and instead of running back and forth to the brook or well, a line would be formed reaching the whole distance and the pails full of water would be passed along that line of men and boys from the water supply to the fire. Short ropes individually but tied together in a bucket brigade they put out a fire.

Our Boy Scouts can tell how to save a boy who has broken through the thin ice while skating. Several boys will lie flat on the ice end to end and firmly holding each other push the line to the drowning boy.

Alone you may be short ropes but with one hand in God's you can reach out and help many another to the right way that Jesus tells about.

John Henry Sargent

47   *THE UNKNOWN SCOUT*

Every one has heard of the Unknown Soldier who lies buried in Arlington Cemetery at our national capital while the flag flies at half mast and military sentinels maintain a guard of perpetual honor. But how many of you are familiar with the story of the unknown scout whose good turn was responsible for sending the Boy Scout program across the sea from England to the United States?

William D. Boyce, a Chicago businessman, was in London and looking for a building which he was unable to find because of the dense fog which enveloped the city and made it difficult for a stranger to find his way. He stood hesitantly on a street corner, wondering which way he ought to go, when a boy approached him in the semi-darkness and said, "May I be of service to you?" The American told him the address he was seeking. The boy saluted and said, "Come with me, sir," and quickly led him to the desired place.

Mr. Boyce offered the boy a shilling, but to his surprise the young stranger replied, "No, sir, I am a scout and scouts do not accept tips for courtesies." The man was so impressed by the boy's conduct that he asked him several questions about the scouts. The boy explained the principles on which the organization had been founded by General Robert Baden-Powell and afterwards took him to the headquarters of the British Boy Scout Association where fuller information was given him about the new movement.

After Mr. Boyce returned home he at once started to arouse the interest of other businessmen in what was being done for the boys of England, and on February 8, 1910, the Boy Scouts of America was formally incorporated. From that beginning scouting has spread throughout the country until millions of young men have known its benefits.

In recognition of our indebtedness to the unknown English scout, a large statue of a bronze buffalo was sent to London by our National Scout Council and was erected in Gilwell Park. On it is this inscription:

> To the Unknown Scout Whose Faithfulness in the Performance of the "Daily Good Turn" Brought the Scout Movement to the United States of America.

The simple deed of kindness of the English boy had far-reaching consequences of which he did not even dream. Although his name will never be known, his deed will never be forgotten. His helpful act, extending across the sea, has already been an inspiration to countless people whom he has never even seen.

Walter Dudley Cavert

48   *HOW GOD USES LITTLE PEOPLE*

Long ago the people called Syrians used to make raids upon God's people in the land of Israel. In one of these raids they carried off as a prisoner a little Hebrew girl. She was taken to the house of Naaman, who was a great and famous Syrian general. But this great man was a leper, and that was a terrible affliction. It could not be cured, and in those days there were no hospitals and no leper settlements with doctors and nurses.

Can you picture this little maid living as a captive in a strange home? She was far away from her loved ones and she was very lonely. Of course, she did whatever she was ordered to do, for she had no bright prospects of ever being free again. Did she give way to her feelings and grow more and more gloomy and hard to manage? It would have been natural enough for this slave girl to say to herself: "My master, General Naaman, is a leper, and he is going to die. Well, I'm not one bit sorry. I'm only his slave. If he dies it will be good enough for him." But she did not think that way. She bore her master no ill-will; in fact, she wanted him to be healed.

She remembered that in her country there was a wonderful prophet, a "man of God" who, she felt sure, could cure her master of his leprosy. So she told his wife about this man. She was glad to be helpful.

What happened? Naaman the leper went to see the prophet

Elisha and, after much ado, the general did what the prophet advised, and God healed Naaman as Elisha had promised, and "his flesh was restored like the flesh of a little child, and he was clean." Naaman was filled with gratitude and he confessed that Elisha's God was the true God.

How wonderful was the way God used that little girl! God needed someone to remember him in Syria and to speak for him in Naaman's house. God chose her because she knew him and could tell of his power and love, as no one else in that heathen land could do. She had been taught to love God when she was growing up in her happy home in Israel. Now the opportunity had come to be God's witness, to be a speaker for him. Her captivity, with all the suffering which this little maid could not understand, was a part of God's plan for her. Perhaps later on she saw the reason for it, for her testimony influenced a great general, and also the kings of Syria and Israel, and the prophet Elisha too. And *we* know that what she did has been told and retold for thirty centuries. Think of it!

God will use every willing boy and girl. You do not need to be experienced, or a grownup. What he wants is our love and trust. He will honor and bless the little we do to serve him, if it is our best. So, boys and girls, be encouraged. You have a place in God's heart and he looks to you to be loyal to him by your conduct and your speech. Remember that often from the smallest effort great results can come.

> There's not a child so small and weak
> But has his little cross to take,
> His little work of love and praise
> That he may do for Jesus' sake.

Binney Simpson Black

7. *FRIENDS AROUND THE WORLD*

❦

SNOWFLAKES

Bruce blinked the snowflake from his eyelash, the better to see into the window of Charlie Ting, laundryman. Bruce always stopped for a minute by this window in the hope that some of the Ting children would be playing beside their father.

Yes, there was the small Ting girl, sitting on the floor looking at a picture book. Bruce stared at her and thought, "I'm glad I'm American. I'd hate looking different from the other fellows —slanty eyes and everything. I'm glad I'm me."

Snowflakes fluttered softly on Bruce's face as he walked on toward home. Some fell on the dark sleeve of his jacket. He studied their delicate patterns.

"There'll be enough for snowballs soon," said a voice behind him. Bruce turned and waited for Bert, the son of the Negro doctor.

The two boys walked on together. They talked about the snow, but all the time Bruce was thinking, "I'm glad I'm white. I'd hate looking different from the other fellows—dark skin and everything. I'm glad I'm me."

A boy waved at them from a long shining car driven by a chauffeur in uniform.

"I'm glad I'm not rich," Bruce told Bert as they watched the car drive out of sight. "I'd hate being the only boy in school who rode in that kind of a car—and everything. No wonder the fellows call him a sissy. He's so different."

Bert turned into the road that led to his home, and Bruce walked on alone, thinking how lucky he was to be born himself. He was feeling sort of sorry for all the boys who were different from him. The ones who were too fat and the ones who were too thin, the ones who were too well dressed and the ones who were too shabby, the ones who could not do their schoolwork well and the ones who did it so well that they were called "teacher's pet."

It was seeing Clarence that made him think of the ones who studied so much that they talked like the pages of a schoolbook. Clarence was doing something queer and different, as usual. He seemed to be studying his own mittened hand through a magnifying glass. Bruce stopped beside him to see what he was doing.

"Want to look?" offered Clarence.

Bruce took the magnifying glass and looked where Clarence pointed. It was nothing but a snowflake—but what a snowflake!

"Oh boy! It looks like the pictures of snowflakes in our science readers!" said Bruce.

"Of course, it does!" said Clarence. "Did you think someone dreamed up those pictures? Now look at another snowflake."

Bruce found a single flake on his own mitten. "It's just as lacy and complicated as the first—but different."

"Of course," said Clarence. "You could photograph hundreds of snowflakes and find no two exactly alike."

"But how can things so tiny be so different?" asked Bruce.

"That's just the way God planned the world!" Clarence had his talking-like-a-book voice, but Bruce did not care. "I read the other day that you could not find two maple leaves exactly alike. They look enough alike that you would know they were all from the maple trees, but there would be some little differences—in the outline or the size or the tracery of the veins. They would differ in some little way."

"Like fingerprints," said Bruce. "The little whirls of lines on my fingers are not exactly like those of anyone else in the world."

"Like shells," said Clarence. "There are hundreds of different families that live in shells, but even within each family the shells are different."

"And dogs." Bruce watched a St. Bernard puppy playing with a setter. "We found that out when we lost our Jill and went all over town looking for black cockers. From a distance they all looked like Jill, but close to, every cocker was different."

"The world is much more interesting because things are not alike," said Clarence as he turned up the sidewalk toward his house. Bruce walked on, studying the snowflakes that lighted softly on his jacket or mittens.

"I'm glad God makes snowflakes different," he thought, "and dogs—and shells—and leaves—*and people!*"

Alice Geer Kelsey

50   THE ARTIST'S DREAM

I expect you know a very beautiful picture by Mr. Harold Copping called *The Hope of the World,* which shows Jesus surrounded by a group of children of all nations. Perhaps you have it in your Sunday school room. If so, I am sure you would like to go and look at it again. It is said that when Mr. Copping first painted this picture the faces of all the children were white. Then one night he dreamed about his great picture. He had gone into his studio and was startled to find a stranger busy at work upon it. The visitor had a palette in one hand and a brush in the other. Angrily, he went forward to see what was happening, and to his astonishment found the stranger was painting in the faces of the children. "How dare you touch my picture?" cried the artist.

The stranger looked round with a calm, sad and serious face, and replied: "How dare you use only a white color when you have all these other colors in your hands? Do you not know that these children come from many lands, from many peoples, and cannot possibly all be white?"

Just at that point the artist awoke, and felt deeply the rebuke of the stranger. He proceeded at once to his picture and painted it as we now know it to be, and it has carried its message of the Redeemer's love to the children of all peoples and all races ever since. One can imagine, I think, who that stranger was in the thought of the artist. He must have felt that his Lord himself had taken an interest in that picture.

I wonder if we have learned the lesson that the artist had to learn. Do we really believe the black boys and the yellow girls, the red and the brown, are all brothers and sisters, and that Jesus loves them just as much as he loves us?*

Albert D. Belden

51   *THE VALLEY OF ECHOES*

Many travelers pass through a certain narrow valley with high cliffs on either side. This valley repeats the sounds which are made in it. It is said that even a whisper is re-echoed. So it might well be called Echo Valley. Every person traveling through this valley hears the echo of his own voice. A shout, a song, a whistle, the crash of a falling tree, the rumble of a sliding rock, are repeated as the echo comes from the stone walls of the valley.

One day two hunters pitched their tent in this valley. As they drove the stakes into the ground, one of them accidentally hit the other's thumb. This gave him great pain and in a loud, angry voice he shouted, "Curse you!" His angry shout disturbed the quiet valley and from the walls came the echo in just as angry a tone, saying, "Curse you!"

Through this valley came an old bearded man making his way over and around the boulders. He was in search of gold. Over one shoulder he carried a pickax, and in his hand he had a shovel. He was a miser, hoarding gold. He lived all alone in a small shack in the next valley, and having no one to whom to talk he talked to himself. That day, looking at the rocks in search of gold, he said to himself over and over again, "I want gold; I want gold." And in the valley could be heard the echo, "I want gold; I want gold."

A man who was running away from everything, from his family and friends, decided to live all alone in this valley. He believed that his friends had treated him cruelly, that he had been cheated and wronged by everyone. He was filled with anger and hate. The first night in the valley the deep quietness got on his nerves. He could not sleep. He thought only of all the people he hated. He got up and shouted into the darkness, "I hate you!" And through the stillness of the night came the echo, "I hate you!"

An artist had heard about the beauty of this valley. He came a long distance in order to spend a few days here to paint pictures. He could not find words to express the beauty he beheld. He said that such beauty could not be expressed in words but only in a picture such as he intended to paint. Looking at the gorgeous colors of the sunset on his first day in the valley, tears of joy came to his eyes, his heart beat faster and warmer, and in his great happiness he said, "I love this beautiful world, the God who made it, and the people who are in it." And from the walls of the valley came the echo repeating, "I love this beautiful world, the God who made it, and the people who are in it."

This valley is like the world in which we live. The hunter who said, "Curse you!" heard the echo calling back to him, "Curse you!" If we curse others, they in turn will curse us. The Bible says, "With what measure ye mete, it shall be measured to you again" (Matt. 7:2), which means that we are paid back in kind, or as we sometimes say, "We get a dose of our own medicine." Furthermore, the Bible says, "Curse not!"

The old man who said, "I want gold," heard the echo say the same thing. In that way also the valley is like the world. One says, "I want money, I want gold," and others answer, "I want money." So people scramble for money, and in their haste forget about the better things of life. The Bible tells us that the love of money causes much trouble.

Look at the man who shouted, "I hate you!" The valley shouted back, "I hate you!" That is the way it is in life. If we hate others, they will hate us. God tells us very definitely in the Bible that we are not to hate anyone.

The artist saw the beauty in that valley. He loved God, other people, and this world in which God had put him. He cried out, "I love you," and the valley cried back, "I love you." Life is like that. If we say, "I love you," others will say to us, "I love you."

If we look angrily at others, they will look the same way at us. If we smile, others will smile back. Jesus said, "Thou shalt love the Lord, thy God . . . and . . . thy neighbor as thyself," (Matt. 22:37, 39).

Everything we do and say in life has an echo. If we are evil-thinking, selfish, and hating persons, the echo of that badness comes back to us. If we are kind, generous and loving, the echo of that goodness comes back to us.

Jacob J. Sessler

52   MOVING IN A CIRCLE

Then the seventh angel blew his trumpet, and there were loud voices in heaven, saying, "The kingdom of the world has become the kingdom of our Lord and of his Christ, and he shall reign for ever and ever."   REVELATION 11:15 (RSV)

It was a great day for Jim. His mother told him that he was big enough to go to the county fair, all by himself. And she gave him a dollar bill to spend just as he pleased. It did not take him long to be on his way for an afternoon of high adventure.

When he returned home that evening for supper, he did not have much to say to his mother about animal exhibits and car shows. He had even less to say about machinery displays and model buildings. All he talked about was the merry-go-round. That had attracted him more than everything else.

As he watched the boys and girls riding the brightly colored horses to the gay tune of the little pipe organ, he was thrilled. He thought, "That's the life for me." So he took one ride and then another until all of his money was gone.

Jim's mother was disappointed in his report. She had expected him to see something worth while as well as amuse himself. But all he had done was to ride on the merry-go-round. She scolded him for wasting his time. "You rode all afternoon," she said, "and got nowhere. You stopped just where you started."

The lesson Jim learned that day stuck with him. Even when he was a grown-up man he remembered that boyhood experience on the merry-go-round. How tragic it is, thought Jim who had now become a man, that life is nothing more than a ride on a merry-go-round for many people. They are wasting not merely an afternoon but a whole lifetime. They're just going round and round in a circle and getting nowhere.

Yet can we ever break away from our circle? We can't always go straight ahead, Jim thought, for there are some things that we have to do over and over again. We eat and sleep, work and play, day in and day out. When we do that we are moving in a circle and we'll never escape from it.

But then a new idea flashed in his mind. He thought of a different kind of circle. This circle is not like a merry-go-round in which everything goes round and round, always moving in the same track. This circle is like a spiral; it's shaped like a cone, an ice-cream cone. Going in one direction it becomes smaller and smaller, but going in the other direction it becomes larger and larger. If life is like a spiral, it is not a bad thing to go around in a circle. The important thing is the direction in which we are traveling.

If the good life is to grow in us, we must move so that the circle becomes larger and larger. We must be interested in more and more things and more and more people. Our circle must include not only the people who are like us; it must be enlarged to take in people of other races and nations. Finally, the spiral becomes so large that it takes in the whole world. Then it becomes like the hymn, written by Frederick L. Hosmer:

> Thy kingdom come, O Lord,
> Wide circling as the sun;
> Fulfill of old Thy word
> And make the nations one.

And it is like the vision which is reported to us in the Book of Revelation, when all the people in heaven become joyful because all the men and the nations of the earth are united in one big circle, the kingdom in which Christ rules over all.

Karl H. A. Rest

53　　　　　*NO MORE SEA*

Jerry was ten. Or to be quite exact, Jerry was ten and a half. He was always exact about it himself, and did not like people to forget the half. After all, he was nearly eleven.

And Jerry lived by the seaside. In the summer he spent all his free time on the beach, or in the sea. When the wind was blowing and the sea was covered with waves that came rolling up the beach in a flurry of foam, Jerry used to dive into the breakers, or let them curl and break over him as he sat back into them. And on calm days he practiced his swimming strokes, or dived down to the sandy bottom of the sea exploring among the stones and the shells.

On the beach he constructed pools, and little harbors, and made model ships which sailed in the little world he had made for himself. He collected white stones, and pink shells, and dried starfish. . . . When he found a flat stone he would throw it out to sea, making it skim and skip across the water. Once he made a stone skip ten times, once for each year of his life, and he said that when he was eleven he would make one skip eleven times.

One Sunday, when Jerry was in church, he heard the minister read from the Book of the Revelation, which Jerry knew was the very last book in the Bible. The writer was describing a kind of dream of a new world that he had seen. Jerry listened carefully. He heard the minister read, "And there was no more sea" (Rev. 21:1).

At dinner that day Jerry said, "I hope the world doesn't come to an end yet."

"Why not?" asked Mother.

"Because when it does come to an end there will be a new world without any sea, and I don't think I'd like a world without any sea. In fact, I'm sure I shouldn't."

Then Daddy laughed, and said: "No, and I don't think I should either. The sea is fun."

But Daddy went on to tell Jerry why St. John had dreamed of a world without a sea. He told him that St. John was a prisoner on a little island. He had been put there because he was a Christian. But his friends were all on the mainland. Over there, beyond the sea, some of his friends were suffering, in prison and worse, because they also were Christians. And St. John loved them, and wanted to be with them in their suffering, so that he might comfort them and help them.

It was the sea which divided St. John from these friends.

Other friends of his were on the mainland doing just the kind of work St. John himself had always done, and which he still wanted to do. They were telling people that God loved the world so much that he had sent his Son into the world to help it. Because the love of God was in their hearts they were telling this good news in all the towns on the mainland. And St. John wanted to be with them to share their great work.

It was the sea which divided St. John from his friends.

When Daddy had told Jerry about St. John, Jerry was very quiet for a long time. That afternoon Jerry went down to the beach, and sat down on the sand, and hugging his knees he looked far out to sea, the sea that he loved, the sea that was fun. And in his heart he was sorry for St. John, who had also looked at the sea and wished it was not there. He knew then that real people, grown-up good people, like his Daddy and Mummy, were fair and just because they tried to see things from the other person's point of view. Daddy thought the sea was fun, but he also knew that it was no fun for St. John on his prison island.

But still the sea was fun. Jerry looked at the ripple of the waves on the beach, and he looked far out where the horizon met the sky. He could never hate the sea. He wanted it to be there always and for always. It was not the sea that was bad, it was bad men who made it horrid. If only all men loved good things, and loved people properly, then God's world would be a new world, and the sea would never be like a prison wall. Perhaps, after all, that was what St. John meant. There would not be that kind of sea any more, but the whole world, the earth, the yellow sands, the cliffs and rocks, and the sky, and the dear old sea would be fine for everybody to enjoy.

Then Jerry said a little quiet prayer in his heart, and asked God to help him never to spoil any part of God's world for other people, but to help them to be happy in it always.

C. J. Buckingham

54   *THE BOY WITH MANY FRIENDS*

A man that hath friends must show himself friendly: and there is a
friend that sticketh closer than a brother.   PROVERBS 18:24

There is a celebrated picture with this rather curious title,
The Boy with Many Friends. The artist has shown us what may
well have been a familiar scene in a boarding school in olden
days. The boys are gathered together in the schoolroom, but
lessons are over and something rather exciting is happening.
The principal figure of the picture is a rather shy-looking boy.
He does not seem the sort of boy who at most times would
attract much notice; but in the picture he is the very center of
attention. Everyone is making up to him. And the reason is not
far to seek. On the floor stands a large hamper. It has just been
opened and from the midst of straw and paper have been taken
cakes and fruit and all manner of good things. It is this boy, the
owner of the hamper, who is the boy with many friends. But
most of his would-be friends look as if they are only offering him
their friendship for the sake of what they can get out of him,
while the expression of embarrassment on the boy's face shows
that he is wondering how much of the contents of the hamper he
will get for himself when all this professed friendship has
achieved its purpose.

Now, to that picture I want to add a story. This time it is a
little girl who is the central figure. One day a good friend of
mine went to stay at her house. She soon became friends with
him. Presently she asked, "Do you like dollies?"

"Yes, very much," was the reply.

"Then I'll show you mine."

Thereupon she brought out a whole family of dolls, and a very worthy and respectable family it was. Of course, my friend admired each one as it appeared, and when they were all standing in a row he asked, "And now tell me, which is your favorite dolly?"

The little girl paused. Then she said: "There's one more you haven't seen yet. She's my favorite." Then she paused again before she said, "Do you really like dollies very much?"

"Why, yes," my friend answered. "Don't you see how interested I am in all these? They are such a splendid lot."

"But *she* isn't splendid," said the little girl. "You're quite sure you like dollies, and will you please promise not to smile if I show you my favorite?"

My friend solemnly promised. Then the little girl went to the cupboard again.

"Here she is," she said. And she held out the most tattered and dilapidated old doll that ever was! Its hair had come off, its nose was broken, its cheeks were scratched, it was short of several limbs.

"Well, well," said my friend, taking the poor old thing gently in his hands, "and why do you like this one best?"

"I love her most," said the little girl, "because if I didn't love her, no one else would."

So you see the doll with few friends had at least one good friend.

Now, thinking of that picture, *The Boy with Many Friends*, and then of this story, here are two things worth remembering about our friendship.

One is that we must never make our friends or use our friends just for what we can get out of them. I know that we should never dream of doing that purposely. The picture I have spoken of is nearly one hundred years old, and I am sure no decent fellows would behave like that at school today. But, for all that, it is easy to slip into the way of being friendly with folk just as long as they are useful to us or interest us, and then dropping them. There is no real friendship to be found in that way. Friendship is a matter of giving as well as taking.

The other thing to remember is that one of the most blessed things we can do is to offer our friendship to those who have not got many friends. "Friend of the friendless" is one way in which Jesus has been described. It is a very beautiful description. And if we also can keep a look out for those who do not have many friends, and modestly but sincerely offer them our friendship we shall be doing one of the best things we can do in life.

R. E. Thomas

55   THE OLDEST THING IN THE WORLD

Love is of God.   1 JOHN 4:7

What is the oldest thing in the world? When we talk about something being very old, we say it is as old as Methuselah. How old was Methuselah? He was the oldest man that ever lived and the Bible tells us that when he died he was nine hundred and sixty-nine years, nearly a thousand years, old. But there are many things older than a thousand years. Trees are sometimes older than that and a piece of coal is thousands of years older. The Bible is older than a thousand years, so are the mountains, and the sea and the sky and the Atlantic Ocean. There must be something older than any of these things. Can you guess what it is?

The Oldest Thing in the World

The other day I went into a big store to see if I could see the oldest thing in the world. Yes! I went to the toy room and watched the children. I watched the boys with the mechanical toys and the airships and submarines, the radio and the block signal systems and the walking elephants, and yet I was not sure that I saw the oldest thing in the world. Then I watched the girls. There was one little girl and she was holding a doll that had real eyelashes, and folded her hands and went to sleep, and after I had watched her for a little while, I knew that I had found the oldest thing in the world.

Can you guess? No! It is not curiosity. No! It is not play. It is love. The love of a little girl for her doll is older than mountains or trees, or rocks and oceans. Love is the oldest thing in the world, for God, who lived before mountains or oceans, or trees, or dolls, is love, and love is of God.

Let me tell you how old love is. The other day some men were digging in an old land called Egypt and they found the body of a little girl. It had been wrapped in spices and linen so carefully that it had not been destroyed and when they unwrapped the linen, what do you think they found? A little doll. The little girl thousands of years ago had loved her doll just as the children today, and thousands of years after, men found the doll still in her arms.

And if you go back and back and back, before the world was made, and before the angels, you will find love, for you will find God and God is love. The Bible tells us quite plainly that our love is born of God's love. It tells us that "we love because he first loved us." Our love for birds and flowers and little children, and for father and mother, brother and sister, and for God himself, is but the fruit of his great love for us.

Friends Around the World

Whenever you see a little girl playing with a doll, remember that love is not only the greatest thing in the world but also the oldest thing in the world.*

Hugh Thomson Kerr

8. LEARNING TO SHARE

✤

An angel was visiting a city, observing people without being observed. One night he noted a hungry newsboy fallen asleep. A young lady came along with a male companion. Seeing the newsboy, she shyly in her pity dropped a sixpence into his pocket and was coming away when the young man with her gave another sixpence and an old lady standing by gave threepence and another young man, though not very heartily, handed in a shilling. So that, after all had been quietly slipped into the little sleeper's pocket, he had received two shillings and threepence. Delighted, the angel flew away to notify the great recording angel about the good deed he had just witnessed. "I know, I know," said the recording angel, "see, it is all written down already, as the Lord told me," and he showed him the book. But there was only ninepence recorded, "Because," as he went on to explain, "that young maiden gave sixpence out of her love, and the aged lady gave threepence out of pity, but the young escort gave because he wanted to be thought well of by the young lady, and the other young man gave because he did not want to be thought mean. These last two do not count."

Ralph W. Sockman

57 THE BUILDING OF ST. SOPHIA

There was once a great emperor who determined to build a church which should be even more lovely and wonderful than Solomon's Temple, and he determined to build it all by himself. He did not think how he could please God by his gift, nor how he could best help the people to praise him there. His heart was full of pride, and he thought only of how men would praise him for the wonderful building, and how God would thank him when he reached heaven. So he ordered it to be cried through the city: "Justinian, the Emperor, will build a church alone. Let no one offer gifts."

Day by day the church grew, its great pillars and high arches, its marble benches, the great dome, and the roof covered with gilded tiles. There were wonderful colored pictures inlaid in the marble, angels with spread wings, the twelve apostles, and one of Jesus throned and crowned. There were silver and gold in the church—beautiful silver and gold, and jewels—beautiful curtains, and lamps that sparkled like rubies in the darkness. On the slab over the door by which people should come in were carved these words: "This church to God, Justinian, Emperor, gave."

Now, far away in that city, in a little cottage by the sea, there lived a poor old widow, so lame that she could hardly ever get about, and so poor, she could only just keep herself alive. She had heard people talking, as they passed her window, of the great church which was being built, but she did not hear the heralds crying: "Justinian, the Emperor, will build this church alone. Let no one offer gifts." She was ill in those days, and a little bird used to sit on her window and sing. It seemed to her that God had sent it, and she longed to offer him some gift as a thanksgiving. But what had she to give?

One day, as she lay by the window, she saw the great oxen which pulled the carts full of heavy marble for the building of the emperor's church struggling up the street. The oxen were dragging the marble from the ships which brought it to that great city from far lands to a place where it would be hewed into great square blocks for building. They looked thin and hungry.

A beautiful thought came into Euphrasia's mind. She would help the oxen to pull better, and that should be her gift to God. So she took some straw from the poor thin mattress where she lay and held it out for the oxen to eat. The bed was harder to lie on after that, but her heart was happy. She had helped in praising God.

The great day came when the church was to be dedicated. A long procession moved through the streets—soldiers in polished armor, flag-bearers with crimson-and-golden banners, and in the center, on a milk-white horse, the emperor himself. "Lift up your heads, O ye gates, and be ye lifted up, ye everlasting doors, and the King of Glory shall come in," sang the choir inside. Back swung the silver doors, and in passed the emperor and all his people.

Justinian looked proudly round the wonderful church, and then turned to the stone over the door. On it were written these words: "This church to God, Euphrasia, widow, gave!"

The emperor gave a cry of anger. The choir stopped their singing. The trembling sculptor came forward and fell at Justinian's feet. "Sir, those are not the words I carved," he said.

"Who is Euphrasia?" asked the Emperor, and, turning to one beside him, "Go, fetch her here to me," he said.

Into the great church there came Euphrasia in her poor ragged dress, walking with a stick because of her lameness.

"Euphrasia," said the emperor, "how dare you disobey my command that none should offer gifts for this church!"

"Why, it was nothing," she answered. "I did not know that you would be angry. I had been ill, and when God made me well again I wanted to offer him a gift to show that I loved him. So I gave some of the straw on which I lie, to the oxen that pulled the marble from the ships. Sir, I did nothing more."

"Look!" said the emperor, pointing. "Read above that door. Your gift was small, but it was a gift of love, and God has accepted it. Mine was a gift of pride, and God does not want it."

Then the great emperor turned to the poor lame widow and said: "Euphrasia, may God help me to grow in love and goodness, so that in heaven I may praise him with you."

Vera E. Walker

58   *THE MAGIC VIOLIN*

It is more blessed to give than to receive. ACTS 20:35

One day some elders of the church at Ephesus had walked down to Miletus, a seaport, to talk to Paul who was on board a ship sailing to Jerusalem. While he was talking to them, he remembered something that Jesus had said but which you cannot find in the four gospels. It is a word that has been passed from man to man but has never been written down by any of the writers of the life of Jesus. Sometime, somewhere, Jesus had said, "It is more blessed to give than to receive." Paul gave this word to the elders as a sort of motto for them to think about as they walked back home.

There was once a little prince who had all sorts of wonderful playthings. Nice things to eat, fine clothes to wear, servants to wait on him and ponies to ride. The king and queen—his father and mother—were always thinking what they could do to make this little prince happy. They were always giving him something new but he never seemed to be happy very long. He soon tired of the things he had and grew cross and peevish and wanted something else. Men were sent to far-off countries to bring back whatever they might find of things strange or rare or beautiful which they thought the prince would like. They brought curious kites from China, baby elephants from India, ponies from the Shetland Islands, tiny canocs from the South Seas, and all manner of mechanical toys and pet animals. But the prince played with them for an hour or two and then he became unhappy again. People were brought in to play all kinds of muscial instruments and to dance before him. Magicians and acrobats performed wonderful feats. He had all the sweetmeats and cakes he could eat but nothing seemed to please him for very long. He soon tired of everything.

At length, a very wise man came to court and the king and queen asked him to help them make their boy happy. He looked over all the playthings and all the other possessions of the prince very carefully. Finally, he said, "There is something among these things which is bewitched and the prince cannot be happy while he has it." But the wise man could not, or would not, tell them which one of the things was enchanted.

"All these things must be gotten rid of," said the wise man.

"He must give them all away and then the bad charm will be broken."

Next morning, a herald went into all the towns around about calling the children to the palace so that the prince could give them his toys. You may be sure there was a big crowd at the palace gate the next morning. Laughing and jostling one another, the children waited for the prince to come out. His servants brought out loads and loads of toys and gave one to every boy and girl there. Such laughter there was, such shouting! Such whirring of rattles, such tooting of trumpets and thumping of drums! Never before had the children seen such wonderful things as were given to them that day. You would have thought the prince would have been happy, wouldn't you? But, when it was all over, while he had more color in his pale face, and more brightness in his eyes than had been seen there for many a day, the evil spell was not broken. In a few hours, he was dull and sad and miserable again.

When the wise man was sent for and told what had been done, he said, "That will not break the evil spell. The prince must give his presents, himself, one by one to the children, and give just the thing that suits each child."

So the next day the prince started out with his tutor calling at house after house, giving each child the very thing he wanted most. Soon they came to a house, where they found a poor lame boy who dearly loved music, but he had no instrument to play. He had long wanted a violin but he was too poor to buy one. The prince at once saw that the poor, crippled boy could make fine use of his lovely violin which had come from Italy. Now it happened that the prince was more fond of that particular violin than of any other one of his instruments.

He hesitated. He did not like to part with it. But when he looked at the poor boy again and saw his pale face and saw how eager he was to have the wonderful violin, he ran back to the palace as fast as he could and fetched his favorite toy and gave the violin to the crippled boy.

From that very day the prince grew strong and merry. The enchantment was broken, for he had learned that just what Jesus said was very true: "It is more blessed to give than to receive."

Guy L. Morrill

59   BLACK SHEEP

Are you a black sheep? I hope so. But not the kind we mean when we say, "Oh, he is the black sheep of the family." I wouldn't want you to be that kind of black sheep. I hope you are a black sheep like the one described in the old nursery rhyme:

> Baa, baa, black sheep,
> Have you any wool?
> Yes, sir, yes, sir,
> Three bags full.
> One for my master,
> One for my dame,
> One for the little boy,
> Who lives down the lane.

That little sheep owned three bags of wool. We all own things: clothes, books, tools, toys, homes, talent, and, above all, a fine Christian faith.

Our little black sheep had good common sense. He planned

what he wanted to do with his possessions. Sensible boys and girls make plans, too. First, the sheep planned to give one bag of wool to his master. He had given the sheep a home and food. The sheep was grateful and wanted to express his thankfulness. Second, he remembered his master's wife. She had been kind to him. The sheep wanted to show her his appreciation. Last, the sheep thought of the little boy who lived down the lane. Why give the little boy a bag of wool? What had he done for the sheep? Perhaps he had done nothing. But the sheep was goodhearted and wanted to make the little boy happy.

Jesus once asked, "How much then is a man better than a sheep?" (Matt. 12:12) Each of us should remember the little black sheep, and try to do as well as he did. Every time we give our offering in church we are giving our "three bags full." Our gift is given to the Master, Jesus Christ. Our gift helps to maintain our own church home. And when we give a portion goes to help little boys and girls who live down the lanes both in our country and across the seas.

E. Paul Hovey

60   *GIMME*

It is more blessed to give than to receive. ACTS 20:35

One of the first words that most boys and girls learn is a word which you will never find in a dictionary. It is a short, five-letter word, spelled G-I-M-M-E. A little boy or girl stretches out eager hands and says, "Gimme." When we grow up, we make two words out of the one word. We say, "Give me." But we mean the same thing.

Jesus told a story about a man whose trouble began with those words. This young man had a father, Jesus said, and to his father he said, "Give me my share of your money. I don't want to wait until you die. Give it to me now." The young man was old enough to know better, but still he was using that strange little word. "Gimme," he was saying, "gimme, gimme, gimme."

Do you remember what happened to that young man? Into a bag he put all the money his father gave him, and off he went to have a good time. He took a trip to a foreign country and he wasted his father's money. Finally he had to get a job, but the only work he could find was feeding pigs. At times the young man was so hungry that he felt like eating the food he was supposed to give the animals.

In the New Testament there is another man who said, "Gimme." He was one of Jesus' disciples, but Jesus did not move fast enough for him. Jesus was content to be humble, and he never seemed to care whether people thought he was a great man or not. But this man wanted to have power and honor and influence. At last he could stand it no longer. He went to the officials of that country. He said to them, "Give me thirty pieces of silver, and I will betray Jesus into your hands. I'll take you to the place where he is, and you'll have no trouble arresting him."

That man's name was Judas, and do you remember what happened to him? He realized too late what evil thing he had done. So he went back to the priests. "I have done wrong," he said. "Take back your money and set Jesus free." But the priests would not listen to him. And Judas, the man who had said "Give me" once too often, went out and hanged himself.

Whenever a person makes "gimme" the law of his life, he becomes like a pool of water that has no outlet. He grows stagnant. Everything good in him dies. If we really want to live happy and contented lives, we must give as well as get. We must become like a lovely lake which has an inlet on one side, where the cold mountain streams pour in their clear, clean water, and an outlet on the other side, where the lake itself overflows and sends out its own water to give life to the valleys below. The only life we can save is the life that we spend. Jesus said, "It is more blessed to give than to receive." You will be happier when you give than when you say, "Gimme."

Roy M. Pearson

61   *WHAT THE CHILDREN GAVE TO GOD*

One rainy Sunday afternoon, two children had difficulty entertaining themselves until they stumbled on the idea of acting out their Sunday-school lesson of the morning. The little boy agreed he would be Noah and his sister could be Mrs. Noah. They found an old cardboard box which they decided would be an ideal "ark," so they started to fill it with their animals. The bathtub seemed the logical place for their "flood." They turned off the electric light, and the "sun" disappeared. Then they turned on the shower, and the floods descended. After some time they turned off the shower, and the rains ceased and the ark floated on the waters. They pushed the wall switch, and the sun reappeared. They pulled the plug of the bathtub, and the floods descended until the ark once more rested on dry ground.

There was another part to the story, however. Noah and his wife had offered a sacrifice to God. The children decided the kitchen stove would be the place for them to burn their sacrifice. Reaching into the ark the little boy found one of his sister's animals and said, "Let's burn this. It would make a good gift for God."

"Oh, no," said his sister in alarm, "I couldn't part with that." Then reaching in the ark she found one of her brother's animals and said, "Here, let's give this to God instead."

Her brother was unwilling to agree to that. They pondered for some time and then the little girl had a happy thought. Scampering off to the attic she returned in a few minutes with a little toy lamb. It had only three legs, its head was smashed, it had no tail, and it was so dirty no one could have guessed its original color. "Here," she cried, "let's give this to God. We will never want it again."

Her brother agreed, so they made their sacrifice. The little broken lamb they did not want was given to God.

Charles H. Hagadorn

62   THE STORY OF A CHURCH DOLLAR

Have you ever heard about the church dollar and what it did? It was just one little dollar, and it looked for all the world just like its brothers and sisters, of whom there were so many millions in the world.

One Sunday morning there came into the church some pennies and nickels and dimes and quarters. They came in all sorts of ways, some in church-school envelopes, some in deep pockets, some tied up in the corner of a handkerchief, some in little mite boxes. They all arrived in the offering plate together. There they opened their eyes and looked around.

"Here we are," they said, "ninety-eight, ninety-nine, one hundred—a whole dollar." Then they joined hands and sang a little song of thanksgiving for the sheer joy of being alive. So the happy church dollar was born.

Pretty soon, however, the church dollar stood up and looked around.

"My, there is much to do, for this church is a very busy place, and there are many things to be taken care of. How grand it is to have a part in what the church is busy with! Let us get to work and help."

So they divided into companies, pennies and nickels and dimes and quarters, and off they went. Some went into the pulpit to open the Bible and lead in worship and preach a sermon. Others hastened to the choir loft to sing a song of praise and play the organ. Still others hurried down to the cellar to put fuel in the furnace so that the people would not be cold when they came to worship. A little group went into the church school to make the boys and girls comfortable and to get some Bibles and lesson papers for them to use. Some very practical pennies and nickels found scrub pails and sweepers and started to clean up the building; with hammer and nails began to mend a broken porch step, and with paintbrushes began to give the dirty walls a fresh coat of paint. Surely there was a great deal for a dollar to do.

But some of these pennies and nickels and dimes and quarters had sharp eyes and good memories. "You know," they said, "we are church coins and the Christian church is a very big church; in fact, it goes all the way round the world. We ought to go as far as our church goes, and help in all that it is doing." So those who were not busy in the home church divided themselves into squads and went out, north, east, south, and west, all over the world.

The Story of a Church Dollar

Some went into other towns near by where there were small churches and church schools that needed their help to open the Bible and preach the sermon and put coal on the fire. Some went into the southern mountains where the people have very poor schools and churches; others to the big cities where people live in crowded houses, and into the big forests where the lumbermen work, and to the western plains where Indian villages are, and even into the Rocky Mountains and beyond.

Some of these coins took ship and sailed across the sea as far as Japan to visit our missionary, and to Persia, where another friend of ours is running a hospital, and into Korea, India, Syria, South America and Africa. The sun never sets on that dollar.

A few pennies and nickels and dimes took a train to the national headquarters and came to a great building where the Board of Christian Education lives, so that they might help that Board do something for the many young people in our colleges, to provide books and lesson papers for the church schools all over the country, to organize schools where there were none, to help the young men who are going to become ministers to get an education.

A little group of pennies and nickels went off into a quiet corner where there were some old ministers and widows of ministers, to give them a bit of help and cheer.

Such a busy dollar that was, with not an idle moment on its hands. It seems as if there was entirely too much for one little dollar to do. It would have been a very discouraged dollar had it not been for its millions of brothers and sisters, all helping with the same work.

That church dollar worked so hard that soon it was all spent, and there was nothing left of it. But it was very happy, because it left behind a very thankful church, and I am glad to say that many more dollars were born in the offering plates to take its place.

The next Sunday the minister preached a sermon from the text, "He that loseth his life . . . shall find it" (Matt. 10:39), and I am sure that church dollar became a great and worthy dollar because of the way it spent its life.*

Herbert K. England

63   WHO OWNS THE LIGHTHOUSE?

That good thing which was committed unto thee keep by the Holy Ghost which dwelleth in us.   2 TIMOTHY 1:14

The man who keeps the light burning in the lighthouse is called the lighthouse keeper. He never is called the owner. The lighthouse does not belong to him; he is in charge of it. His responsibility is faithfully to see that the lighthouse fulfills the intended purpose of its owner.

The lighthouse belongs to the government. It was not built for the lighthouse keeper; it was built to help the sailors and their ships, along the dangerous coast.

The great nation that watches that coast is concerned to protect the lives of all seamen and to save their ships from loss by shipwreck. The nation is, of course, also concerned to see that the lighthouse keeper is cared for. It wants to do all it can to make him safe and fit. It will send him his supplies of food and other necessities, to make him comfortable and keep him efficient, so that he may fulfill his commission to keep the lighthouse.

This is the stewardship way of looking at life. All we have—

our talents—our skills—our money—all possessions are ours, only to handle. We are not the owners of them. We, like the lighthouse keeper, are their caretakers for God. We administer them all for him that they may accomplish his purpose for men and for the Kingdom of God.

Paul said, "Ye are not your own. For ye are bought with a price: therefore glorify God in your body, and in your spirit, which are God's" (1 Cor. 6:19-20). The lighthouse keeper is no more responsible for the light under his care, than you for all the things God has given you to handle and manage.

Jesus said, "Let your light so shine before men, that they may see your good works, and glorify your Father which is in heaven" (Matt. 5:16).

Your light which you must keep shining—just as the lighthouse keeper keeps his particular light shining—may be musical talent, executive skill, speaking ability, legal insight, mechanical dexterity, medical expertness, physical prowess or any one of a myriad other possessions. God wants your special gift, your personal possession, to shine that all men may be helped and profit by it. You are not the owner but the keeper of this light of yours. You are a commissioned administrator for God. You have the gift from him for yourself and for all his children.

As God's appointed keeper, it is your job, in your place, to see to it that each God-owned and God-entrusted possession performs the exact and complete service God intended for it.

The lighthouse keeper's one great concern is that the light shines, in fair and stormy weather, far out to sea that sailors and ships may reach their desired havens. So must we, as good stewards, make all we are and all we have to do his service who owns them all and us as well.

David Livingstone once said all this in an oft-repeated word,

"I will place no value on anything I have, or may possess, except in its relation to the Kingdom of God."

There are many ways in which men fail to be good keepers of their lights, for God. Some deny their stewardship altogether, they put their light "under a bushel." They count their possessions as their own, to do with as they wish. They hoard them and selfishly use God's gifts, and their light is hidden, so that many, whom God intended to walk in their light, stumble and fall and lose their way, because the light is "under a bushel."

Some are careless and unfaithful stewards. They fail to keep their lamps trimmed and filled with oil and often their light burns low or their lamp goes out altogther and there is deep darkness where God intended there should be light.

Let none of us forget, each one is the keeper of his light for God.*

Guy L. Morrill

9. *THIS SINGING WORLD*

❧

64   *A SONG OF THE HEART*

When Franz Joseph Haydn, the Austrian composer, was asked by his friends how it happened that his church music was always of such an animating, cheerful, and even festive quality, he replied: "I cannot make it otherwise. I compose according to the thoughts I feel. When I think about God, my heart is so full of joy that the notes seem to dance and leap from my pen. Since God has given me a cheerful heart I cannot but serve him with a cheerful spirit." His music was literally a song of the heart.

There is a chance for us all to be like that. When we think about God it should fill our hearts with joy. There is a story told of a girl who had very little in life to make her smile. Because of the cares of life laid too early upon her, she was old beyond her years. But she always had a smile for her teacher. When she was asked why she loved her teacher so much, she replied, "Because she is glad to me." For the same reason we should smile and be happy when we think of God, because he has been glad to us.

That is why we should smile and be happy on Easter Day, because it is a symbol of God's gladness to us; because it stands for the happiness of a great and beautiful hope; because it means that we are ever in his love and care and keeping. The spirit of Easter is the spirit of gladness; it is a festival of the springtime;

it is prophetic of new beginning; it holds out a promise of joyous living. If we catch its true spirit and meaning, it will be for us as a song of the heart.

Simeon E. Cozad

65   *MAKING MUSIC*

All boys and girls, I think, like to sing. Even grownups like to sing—if not in the choir, at least in the bathroom.

I want to tell you the story of a boy who had a song in his heart that wouldn't come out. He couldn't sing—at least he could only sing in a squeaky voice. His most precious possession was a pocketknife. He loved better than anything else in the world to whittle away at a stick.

One day, little Antonio—that was his name—and his two special friends, Salvator and Gulio, had a holiday together in the crowded streets of the old town where they lived. It was a special festival day, and all the streets and houses were decorated, the people wore their best, gayest clothes, laughed, met their friends, and had a jolly time.

It was the custom for boys to go and sing on festival days and receive coins from the happy crowds if they pleased them.

Salvator and Gulio stood making their plans. "Come, hurry," said Gulio. "Hurry! The people are generous at festival times. Every minute we lose we are throwing away good money, and we need it badly enough."

And Salvator hurried, for it was true they did need money. They were poor, and their clothes were shabby, even at festival times.

"Do you want to come too?" they called to Antonio, who stood

134

a little way off from them, whittling away at a stick. Antonio looked up. "Yes, I would like to come," he said.

"You certainly cannot sing," they said with giggles, as they remembered Antonio's squeaky voice, "but you can come."

Antonio pondered Gulio's remark as he went along. It made him sad that he couldn't help when the other boys could play and sing. He loved music, too, but he could not make any.

Soon they were in front of the cathedral, and the crowds thronged by. Standing close to Salvator, Gulio put his violin to his chin and began to play. Salvator joined in to sing an old Lombardian folk song.

People listened to the sweet music, and when it stopped they dropped a coin for the young music makers.

"That is a pretty song, lad," said one of them. "Would you sing it again for a lonely old man?"

"Certainly, good sir," said Salvator. Gulio took up his violin and Salvator sang it over again.

The old man put a coin into Salvator's hand, and went on his way. Soon he was lost to sight in the swirling crowds.

Salvator opened his hand, and held up his coin. "Look!" he cried. "A gold piece! A gold piece for a song!"

Antonio came to look at it, and Gulio took it into his hand and held it up to the light. "Truly," he said, "it is a gold piece!" Then, as a second thought, he added: "But he can well afford it. He is the great Amati."

"Who is Amati?" asked Antonio, puzzled. "And tell me, why do you call him great?"

The two boys laughed. "You have never heard of Amati?"

"Of course he hasn't," said Gulio. "What does he know of a music maker; he has no voice, and he is only a whittler. Amati is the great violin maker—the very greatest in all Italy."

With that the two boys ran off home to tell of their good fortune. Antonio followed a long way behind, and very slowly. He was busy with one thought. For quite long enough he had been laughed at for his squeaky voice and his whittling.

Next morning, very early, before anyone was awake, he crept silently out of the house and into the street. In his pockets were some things he had made, and his precious pocketknife. Somewhere in the city the master violin maker lived, and he meant to find him.

At last he stood before his house. Amati's manservant answered his knock, but it was early and he scolded him away. "What do you want at this house?" he cried.

Antonio hung his head and turned away. Then he went up the street a little and waited.

When the sun was well up, Antonio returned and knocked a second time.

This time when the servant opened the door, the great master heard his boyish voice, and followed the servant to the door to see what was wanted.

"I brought these for you to see," said Antonio. "I made them myself with my knife. I want to know if they are good, and if I could learn to make violins?"

The great master smiled down on him, and took into his hands what the boy had brought for him to see.

"Come in," he said.

And Antonio went in to the great master's house.

"What is your name?" he asked.

"Antonio, sir," he said, "Antonio Stradivari."

Then he asked: "And why do you want to make violins?"

"Because I love music," said Antonio, "and I cannot make any. I have but a poor, squeaky voice. You heard Salvator and Gulio play and sing beside the cathedral yesterday."

Then the great master said something that made Antonio very happy. "The song in the heart is what matters. There are many ways of making music. Some can play the violin, some can sing sweetly, some can paint pictures to tell of their joy, some can grow flowers. Each helps to add some loveliness to the world. You are only a whittler, but your song shall be as noble as any."

Antonio never forgot that. He became a pupil of the great Amati. Very early every morning he went to his workshop where he made violins. For weeks and months and years he went. He listened and he learned, until there was not one secret about the making of a violin that he did not know.

By the time he had had his twenty-second birthday his master allowed him to put his own name on a violin he had made. Each instrument had more than seventy pieces. And each one he tried to make more beautiful than the last.

In time he became as famous for his violins as his great master had been. And all his life he kept on making violins. In his little upstairs room, with one side open to the blue sky and the warm, sweet sunshine, he worked away at his happy task— making the very best violins that love and care and skill could make—that today are valued so highly, nearly three hundred years afterwards. He knew that what the great master had told him that first day was true: "The song in the heart is what matters. There are many ways of making music."

That is still true. None of us may be able to sing like Salvator, or play like Gulio, but if we will we can always find some way to let the music out of our hearts.

In a favorite hymn written by M. B. Betham-Edwards is a verse which says:

God make my life a litle song.

Yes, that is the very best way of all of letting the music out of our hearts. All the days—and all our life long! You remember perhaps the rest of the verse:

> God make my life a little song
> That comforteth the sad,
> That helpeth others to be strong,
> And makes the singer glad.

Rita F. Snowden

66   *THE BIRD AND THE STORM*

I will sing a new song unto thee, O Lord. PSALM 114:9

Have you ever been at the seashore in a storm? The wind lashes the waters into waves that look like mountains. The house trembles, and even great trees bend before the fury of the storm. It grows quite dark even at midday, and the roar of the sea is like great guns in the distance.

About two hundred years ago Charles Wesley, a famous writer of many of our loveliest hymns, was watching a terrific storm on the English coast. From the open window of his cottage he saw the waves dashing high on the beach. Now and then a bird would flash past his window, helpless before the blast.

Suddenly a little bird was blown in at the window. It landed in Mr. Wesley's lap, and at first he thought it was dead. He picked up his trembling little visitor, smoothed its feathers, held it against his breast, and began to sing softly the old hymn, "Pull for the shore, sailor."

The storm was quieting down now, and the little bird stopped trembling. It knew it was in the arms of a friend. It began to sing a little song; soon the sun came out again and the bird balanced on the window sill and flew happily home.

But the bird left something beautiful with Mr. Wesley. A lovely hymn was begining to sing in his heart. He went to his desk and wrote what was then a "new song." It is a hymn we all love. If everyone wrote down a list of hymns that he loves, this one would be on nearly every list.

> Jesus, Lover of my soul,
> Let me to thy bosom fly,
> While the nearer waters roll,
> While the tempest still is high:
> Hide me, O my Saviour, hide,
> Till the storm of life is past;
> Safe into the haven guide,
> O receive my soul at last.

Years afterward, someone asked Mr. Wesley how he came to write "Jesus, Lover of my Soul." Mr. Wesley smiled. "A little frightened bird taught me that hymn. It was blown in at my window in a terrible tempest. I held it in my bosom for a while and quieted its fears. When the sun came out it flew happily away. Isn't that just what Jesus does for you and me when we pass through life's stormy weather?"

Charles N. Thorp

67   *THE SONG IN YOUR HEART*

He put a new song in my mouth, a song of praise to our God.
                                        PSALM 40:3

The train, crowded with passengers, was speeding on its way.
Many of these passengers were students on their way back to
school after a Christmas recess. One of the boys suggested that
the people do some community singing. Two of the boys had
brought musical instruments along, one an accordion and the
other a guitar. They seemed to be able to play almost anything,
and so in a few minutes all the travelers were singing popular
hit songs and old favorites. When the students had run out of
ideas, the leader asked for requests.

In the coach were two children, a little girl of five, whose
name was Kay, and her brother, Chuck, who was seven. Kay was
sitting on a friendly student's knee. "I have a song," she said to
the student, and the student called out: "Here is a young lady
who wants her song to be sung."

"Now tell us what you would like us to sing," the leader said
to Kay.

She did not hesitate a second. "Let's sing 'Jesus Loves Me,' "
she said with a sweet smile.

That is a song almost everyone knows, for he has learned it
in Sunday school. The boy with the accordion and the boy with
the guitar struck the first chord and every person in the coach
sang "Jesus loves me, this I know, for the Bible tells me so."

Many songs had been sung that day. They were songs of all
sorts. But the one Kay requested was the best of all because it
reminded everyone of Jesus and his love for them. Songs are

suggestive that way. They bring up memories of long ago. They cause us to recall those times when we sang them. We think of the places and people who were there and of the things that were said and done.

This is what happened with at least three people in the coach that day. Bill was one of them. He was discouraged. Things had not gone well with him and his family. His father was sick and his mother was worried. He might have to give up his job. And they had had such a hard time making a living and keeping Bill in school.

As Bill sang Kay's song, he remembered the church where he used to go to Sunday school and he remembered the teacher he had had as a small boy. She always used to say: "When you have a problem, take it to God in prayer. He cares for you. He knows the answer and he will help you find it too." Bill saw a gleam of light and hope shining down from above and he found good cheer as he rode back to the college campus.

Jim had a different problem. His was a temptation, one that had seemed too strong for his power to resist. His will was weak and the habit of drinking had become so bad that now he frequently made a fool of himself. Of course he was ashamed of himself, but he could not break his habit. Kay's song brought Jim new hope. He remembered his pastor back home and his kindly advice. Dr. Roberts had often spoken from the pulpit of the danger of drinking and had told how it makes a slave of those whose wills are weak. He had said that only God can help a person to break a habit such as Jim's. But Jim had not wanted any advice or any help. Yet, deep down, he knew that only God could give him the strength to win his fight. As he sang Kay's song, he resolved: "Jesus does love me, even if I am often disgusting. He will help me to conquer my bad habit."

Sam was a bully and a braggart. He was always swaggering before the fellows and telling big stories about how important he was. At first he got by with his "act," but soon his classmates began to laugh at him and to poke fun at his stories. When he spoke, the others just hooted. Sam now felt lonely and neglected. He was sure that no one cared for him.

Kay's song made him think. He asked himself why the fellows laughed at him and booed when he made a suggestion. The song made him take a good look at himself. He knew the trouble was with him. He determined to be the kind of person his friends could believe in and like to have around. He decided on that train trip to make friends and not enemies and to be a help and not a hindrance in the future.

Kay's song was just a simple one, but it was a song of the heart and all who sang it found themselves singing it over and over again deep down inside.

Julius Fischbach

68   *THE SECOND VIOLIN*

Whatsoever ye do in word or deed, do all in the name of the Lord
Jesus.   COLOSSIANS 3:17

When Jesus was twelve years old, he began to think that God had a plan for his life—that he was under commission. He said to his mother, "I must be about my Father's business" (Luke 2: 49). He recognized that his business was his Father's business.

A ten-year-old schoolboy was asked by his father, "What is the idea you have in mind, in regard to your violin lessons?"

The boy replied, "For one thing I want to get into God's orchestra."

"So you think," continued his father, "that if you become a good musician, when you die you will go to heaven and sit close to God's throne and play your violin?"

"No," said the boy with a bit of seriousness in his voice, "I didn't mean that at all. God has an orchestra here on earth, and I want to get into it."

"You mean then," persisted the father, "that any person who knows how to make good music gets into God's orchestra?"

"No," replied the boy, "only those who do it with the thought of making people happy and cheerful, those who do it to serve, not those who do it just to make money."

God does have his orchestra here on earth and each one of us has his assigned place to fill. Many of us will not be called upon to play the first violin and have some prominent place to fill; nevertheless, we have our own part to play. It may be a very little part, but it is our part, and should be played in a great way. Thomas Bridges describes an actor as "not a great actor, but an actor who played small parts in a great way." Our second violin in God's plan has a place equally important as the first violin.

Someone has told of a musician who practiced with utmost care upon his trumpet, through a whole day. At evening he dressed in his evening clothes, went to the concert hall, took his place in the orchestra, and never played a single note, as the concert went on and on. Everyone else played—the cornets, the violins, the flutes, the oboes and even the drum, but this man with his well-tuned and polished trumpet played nothing. But he was carefully following the music score all the time. At last, he sat up straighter, his time had come, the moment for which he had prepared. He put his trumpet to his lips and then, all at once, the conductor brought him in. Quick as a flash, clear and true, a trumpet note rang out into the music, commanding and splendid—just one note—no more. Then the man relaxed, his day's work was over. He had rendered his one note, true to time, true to tone. Just at the moment when the orchestra leader called for it, he was there ready to deliver it, ready to do what was assigned him to do, and do it at his best.

It will be serious, indeed, if we think that what we are asked to do is so small that it is unimportant. It is not the size of the job that gives it its deepest meaning, but it is the part it holds in the whole. It is the way we do the job. Be a good second violin, if that is what God has asked you to be.*

Guy L. Morrill

10. OUR FATHER'S WORLD

❧

69 *FLOWERS TURN THEIR FACES TO THE LIGHT*

The Sun of righteousness. MALACHI 4:2

Flowers turn their faces to the light. Did you ever notice that? It is true; and it is a most wonderful thing. If you have never noticed it, you ought to do so. The next time you pass a flower garden, a window box or a flower bed in the middle of a green lawn, just notice how the flowers turn their faces toward the sun. You will notice it especially, I think, in the great yellow flower we call the Sunflower. I suppose it takes its name from the fact that it so plainly and noticeably turns its face to look at the sun. In the morning it faces the east, for there the sun rises. But as the day advances it lifts up its head to gaze in adoration at the sun and follows it across the sky until toward evening it droops its head toward the west, still looking at the great source of light in the heavens. But other flowers do it, too, although oftentimes in them you cannot notice it quite so plainly. But just watch a garden and see if it is not always true that, in so far as they can, flowers turn to face the light.

But I think sometimes you can notice it even more with flowers that are growing in flowerpots inside the house. If your mother has a pot of flowers growing in one of her windows, just notice it the next time you are near it; and I think you will be surprised by the fact that the flowers all turn their faces toward

the glass of the window, for there they get the light, there is the
sun. And that is why your mother has to turn the pot around
ever so often, for all the blossoms look out the window; none
of them faces the inside of the room, and the plant begins to
grow one-sided. For the lovely blossoms have all turned their
faces toward the light. After your mother turns the pot around,
the flowers will slowly—O, so slowly that you cannot see them
do it—turn themselves again and after a few days they will all
be facing the window once more; and your mother will have to
turn the pot around again to see the blossoms.

Malachi 4:2 speaks of "the Sun of righteousness" and we call
Jesus Christ, our Saviour, "the Sun of righteousness"; and just
as flowers turn their faces to the sun in the sky, so human beings,
men and women and boys and girls, should look to this Sun of
Righteousness. For Christ Jesus is just as important to men as
the physical sun in the sky is to flowers. Flowers must have light
and warmth to live and grow. Men must have spiritual light and
spiritual warmth to live the right kind of lives, and to grow
spiritually. And it is just as natural for boys and girls to look
to Jesus, who called himself, you remember, in the New Testament, the "Light of the World," as it is for the flowers to turn
to the sun. You will do that naturally, if you do not let anything
interfere with your look. If you place a screen or pull a window
shade between the flower and the light, of course the flower
cannot turn toward it. If people let sin of any kind interfere,
they cannot turn toward the Light of the World. But with inter-
ference removed, men will turn to Jesus.

Let us never be ashamed of the things we do or say or think
so that we cannot turn to Christ, the Sun of Righteousness, the
Light of the World. That is, let us never allow sin to interfere

with our turning our faces to him. For he gives us life, as the sun gives life to the flowers. He will help us and encourage us. He is the source of the light of the soul. He is the Sun of Righteousness.*

Joseph Anderson Schofield, Jr.

70   *THE MEANING OF FLOWERS' NAMES*

We all like pretty names, but names are useful as well as pretty. If boys and girls had no names, then every time we wanted to speak about someone we should have to describe what he or she looked like. Instead of saying, "Harry is a good boy," we should have to say, "The boy with brown hair and freckles (or ginger hair and big ears) is a good boy." That would be difficult, and it might even be rude. It is much simpler to give Harry a name.

That is why everything has a name. It is why flowers have names. And very often the name a flower has is a name which describes the flower as well. It tells us something about the flower. Or else it is just a pretty-sounding name which suits a pretty-looking bloom. But all names have some kind of meaning.

The Sunflower is easy, for its big face looks rather like the sun, and it always turns its face to look at the sun as well. It would be difficult to think of a better name for that flower.

The Daisy has its name because it opens in the daytime and closes its petals at night just as though it were going to sleep. It is a little Day's Eye. Sometimes it is called a Marguerite, which means a Little Pearl. It looks like a pearl as it grows in the grass, and a Daisy Chain is a very charming kind of pearl necklace.

The Dandelion grows with Daisies, and though it is a pretty flower it can be a great nuisance and gardeners do not like it. They call it a weed, which really is an old English word meaning "a flower." The yellow petals of the Dandelion look like the teeth of a lion. That is what its name means; it is the *"dent de lion,"* the "Lion's Tooth."

Many flowers have Greek names. The Aster looks like a star, and that is what its name means in the Greek language. The Chrysanthemum is the "Golden Flower," and the Anemone is the "Wind Flower," and the Iris is the "Rainbow Flower."

The Primrose appears early in the spring. It has a name which tells us that it is the "Little Firstling."

The Marigold is a great favorite, and it has a lovely name. It is "Mary's Gold," and Mary is the mother of Jesus.

All flowers' names have meanings, though sometimes the name means that the flower was first grown by someone who bore that name. The Begonia was first grown by a botanist named Michel Begon, though there is a type of Begonia called "The Angel's Wings Begonia" which makes us expect something lovely. The Dahlia was first grown by a Swedish botanist named Dahl.

But flowers themselves, as well as their names, have a meaning. They are lovely and when we look at them growing in the fields or in our gardens, filling vases in our rooms, in shop windows or massed on market stalls, they make us feel happy and fresh in spirit and gay of heart. And because God made them grow, that means that God wants us to be gay and fresh and happy ourselves, and to love that which is beautiful. The flowers are God's messengers to us, telling us something about him, and telling us something about ourselves.

C. J. Buckingham

71   *CONSIDER THE LILIES*

> Consider the lilies of the field, how they grow; they neither toil nor spin; yet I tell you, even Solomon in all his glory was not arrayed like one of these.   MATTHEW 6:28-29 (RSV)

Spring is a beautiful season in Palestine where Jesus lived. Travelers tell us that the fields and hillsides are as lovely today as they must have been long ago. There are daisies and buttercups, clover and dandelions, as well as wild flowers which would be strange to our eyes. Among the flowers are the lilies which Jesus loved so much. The fields are full of them. No flower is more common in Palestine than the lily.

The Palestinian lily isn't like our lilies of the valley, nor is it similar to the calla lily, the water lily, or the Easter lily. It is about the size of a daisy. Its center is black and the petals are bright scarlet. The scarlet flames so vividly that Jesus said that King Solomon in his royal robes would not be as gorgeous as the wild lily.

Can you imagine Jesus standing at the foot of a green hill as he taught the people? In the meadows the lilies seemed to dance when the wind stirred them. Time and again Jesus must have exclaimed, "Just *look* at those lilies!"

He was a wonderful Teacher. He would look at a common flower which everyone knew and he would let the flower teach the lessons everyone needed to learn.

"Consider the lilies," the Master said. Let us do just that. What do they tell us? The first lesson is this: *God must love us deeply*. God is our Heavenly Father, and he has given us all that we need for our lives. A world like ours provides all we need for clothes, food and houses. God gave us the flowers, too. These are the "extras." You always know how much somebody loves you by the extra things you are given.

"Look at those lilies," Jesus said. Why? Because *they teach us how to grow.* Everybody likes to grow up. You ask a boy how old he is and he will not say "ten" or "twelve." He always says "ten and a half" or "almost thirteen." Most boys and girls like to measure themselves to see how much they are growing. But we do not grow by fussing about it or by anything else that we ourselves can do. We just grow! We cannot push ourselves up into the air. We must grow as the lilies do. Of course, the seeds must be given a chance. They need nourishment and sunlight. We need those things which help us to grow both physically and spiritually. We need food, sleep and exercise, and we also need truth, love and worship. If our lives are given a chance, they will grow like the lilies.

The lilies also teach us that *we must trust our Heavenly Father.* Flowers have short lives, especially when we cut them. Soon they are thrown away. Palestine lilies last for only about three weeks. Jesus seemed to say: "If God made flowers to be so beautiful for so short a time, if he lavishes care upon these little friends which go away so soon, why not trust him to care for the human children he made, and whom he loves so much more?"

Once there was a traveler called Mungo Park. On one of his trips, he was attacked and robbed by savages. When he was nearly five hundred miles from a settlement, he was so miserable that he almost gave up. Then he saw a tiny moss plant which was no bigger than the tip of his finger. It was perfect in form and beauty. He said to himself: "If God took such care to make a tiny plant and to bring it to perfection in an obscure corner of the earth, he must care for the creatures he made in his own image. He must care for me! I shall trust him." This thought gave him hope, and he was able to keep struggling until he reached safety.

"Just look at those flowers!" They tell us that *the youngest and smallest of us can do helpful things for others.* I know a very little boy, who is just old enough for nursery school. When playing in the field one day, he saw some beautiful flowers. He picked several buttercups and dandelions and a daisy or two. Then he ran to his mother. He didn't know too many words, but when he handed the flowers to his mother she knew that somehow the flowers were speaking to her in their own language. Sometimes what we do for others may seem very small and unimportant. Yet we never can know how much our thoughtfulness will mean to them. The wild lilies were small, but they made the world lovelier and all life sweeter.

David A. MacLennan

72   *NO WEEDS—NO FLOWERS*

Let both grow together until the harvest.   MATTHEW 13:30

There was a man once in Coventry who was worried about weeds. Although I never actually met the man, I know that that was his trouble. It was the weeds in his front garden which worried him most, not that he saw them often but because everyone who passed the house did. His neighbors managed to keep their gardens tidy, but weeds seemed to love his path. They flourished in his flower bed, and his bit of grass seemed to grow twice as fast as anyone else's so that it always needed cutting.

At last, unable to bear it any longer, he determined to do away with those weeds once and for all.

He got into touch with a contractor, asked him to come along and see the garden and then explained what he had in mind. The contractor was a bit staggered.

"Well, yes," he said, "I suppose I could get the stuff and do it. But I'm not at all sure that you'll like it when it is done. It's a bit drastic, you know."

But the worried man stuck to his guns.

And the contractor said they could come and start next week.

Next week they came. There was a truck and three men, with a wheelbarrow, shovels, picks and a roller. They tipped the lorry and out crept a black, tarry, messy mass. Then for two days they worked. They leveled the ground and beat and rolled it hard. Then on top they spread the tarmac and rolled it flat. And that was that! The passers-by, and I, saw it and marveled. There would not be any more weeds there forever.

Yes, but what else? There would not be any flowers there forever, either!

We all like gardens without weeds. But what is a garden without flowers? In Japan, at Kyoto, there is a famous garden which consists of white sand and five low groups of rock. But that is not our English idea of a garden. We have lovely flowers with lovely names, gillies and sweet William, pansies, hollyhocks and love-in-a-mist. We want flowers in a garden and for the sake of the flowers we put up with the weeds, making them as few as we can, but knowing that we cannot possibly get rid of them altogether.

You can see that. I wonder if you can see this? It is a bit harder, but if you think a bit harder you will see it. We would all like a world with only flowers—good, kind, loving people. But can we have it? Can we have a world without weeds—the crooked, the foolish and the bad?

Sometimes we hear people say, "Why doesn't God wipe out all the bad people?" Perhaps, if he did, there could not be any good people either. No weeds, no flowers! No sinners, no saints!

Jesus, of course, did not make it as hard as I do. He told a story and said that God's world was like a farm all sown with wheat. An enemy came and sowed weeds amid the wheat. When wheat and weeds started to grow together, the laborers said, "Shall we get to work and pull up all those weeds?" The Master answered, "No. You would only disturb the roots of the wheat. Leave both to grow together. We will separate them, one from the other, at harvest time."

So it is with us, both good and bad grow side by side in us, in the church, and in the world. God wants flowers, wants our love and help, wants to see us good and kind; but often he has our forgetfulness, meanness and idleness.

Why does not God *make* us good and kind? Would you think much of a present which a friend was *made* to give you? God wants us to offer him the flowers of goodness with love and joy. So, leaving us free to grow them, he leaves us free to grow the ugly weeds too. If we are to be *free,* it must be free to grow both.

So that is why God bears with the weeds and lets the bad go on. It is not because he likes it; he hates it. But he knows that ground that grows weeds can, may yet, grow flowers. So, with wonderful and merciful patience, he waits and waits.

Can it be we who are keeping him waiting for those flowers?

John Wilding

73   *THE IMPATIENT GRAPEVINE*

They that wait upon the Lord shall renew their strength.
ISAIAH 40:31

It was a warm day in the middle of summer and the Grapevine in the garden was feeling rather grumpy. He spoke aloud and said: "I can't understand why I don't begin to do beautiful things like my friends, the trees and the flowers and the vegetables. Here the tulips have all come up and bloomed and gone. I have no beautifully colored blossoms like the tulips, or any of the other flowers for that matter. All I had a few weeks ago were some tiny, green, pinpoint blossoms. They were so small that none of my friends ever noticed I was blooming! Why don't I bear fruit like all my neighbors?"

The Cherry Tree spoke to the Grapevine and said: "Oh, cheer up, it's early yet. Maybe it is not time for you to bear fruit."

The Grapevine answered: "Sure, Cherry Tree, you can talk like that. I remember the wonderful day in the spring when you were filled with beautiful white blossoms. They looked like snow and smelled so lovely in the cool spring evening. Already the pickers have come with their ladders and have picked the beautiful red cherries that grew from those blossoms. How your arms were laden down with that delicious fruit! But look at me, here I am. I just grow here as a vine and whatever fruit I do have looks like a string of green marbles. Nobody wants what I have. Everybody else is giving fruit to help people keep alive and strong and healthy. What is wrong with me? This is the first year that I have been old enough to have blossoms and to give fruit, and nothing happens!"

The Impatient Grapevine

Well, the days went by and soon the end of August was at hand. Still the grapes on the Grapevine were hard and not ready to be picked. The Grapevine again spoke up: "I don't understand. Here all the days of the spring and the warm days of summer have come and gone. Pretty soon, my friend the Robin reminds me, it will begin to grow chilly and winter will be here. Why doesn't my fruit become ripe? I'd like to be helpful like the Apple Tree or the Peach Tree or even my little friends, the Raspberry Bushes."

The Peach Tree spoke up and said: "I'm older than you are, Grapevine, and I remember your mother and your father. They never gave fruit early in the year. You are supposed to wait so that your fruit will be ripe when the touch of frost comes in the air. True, my blossoms did grow into large fruit after the bees buzzed around my branches. But now my fruit is picked for this year. Look at those Raspberry Bushes you were talking about!"

The Raspberry Bushes said: "Yes, look at us! When our fruit was ripe, the girls and boys came every day to pluck it from our fingers. You must remember, though, they did not pick it all the same day. They came back day after day. Suppose all the berries had been ripe on the same day. Goodness, there would have been so many they would not have known what to do. And what if all the other fruits ripened the same week? So you see, it is good that you are able to wait."

So the days went by and as September came the Grapevine made a discovery. The grapes at the tips of his fingers were beginning to turn purple, and sweetness came into them. Then the time came when the grapes were ripe and they had the flavor of the clear crisp days of autumn.

About this time the Farmer came walking through the cornfield, picking the last ears of ripe corn. His little boy was with him, running down the furrow and stopping to pick a cluster of grapes. When he had tasted them he turned to his father and said, "My, these grapes are good!" Then the Grapevine heard the Farmer say, "For the earth bringeth forth fruit of herself; first the blade, then the ear, and after that the full corn in the ear" (Mark 4:28).

The Grapevine said to himself: "Now I am glad that I am not a peach or an apple or even an ear of corn. My fruit helps to show all the beautiful days of the year. Now I will rest so that next year I may bring forth fruit again. I'm glad that all the fruit in the garden does not ripen at the same time."

Robert Newell Zearfoss

74 *THE STRENGTH OF AN ANT*

How strong is an ant? It depends a great deal on the size of the ant. But ants are very strong. I am not sure what is the strongest living thing in the world in proportion to its size, but I venture to say that few things are stronger than ants. Did you ever watch ants at work? It is one of the most interesting ways to spend a warm afternoon. You can learn a great deal, not only about ants, but about working together, and about God. One day, as I was driving along the road, I saw one of the large ant-hills made by the prairie ants. I stopped to watch them at work. These ants pile up the sand sometimes as much as two feet high in a beautifully symmetrical cone. They clear the ground around their home of all kinds of growth, leaving a large bare circle.

I watched these ants at work, coming and going busily, for a time. Then I put a small stone in the mouth of the runway.

The Strength of an Ant

I thought they would try to get it out, and that I could learn how strong they are. I could see the ants at work down below the stone, and I wondered what they were doing. Suddenly the stone dropped out of sight. They had found that it was too large for them to get out; so they dug a hole below it and let it drop down. That was easier than lifting it and carrying it away. I put a bit of a leaf near the opening. One ant picked it up and carried it off. The leaf was several times as long as the ant, and much heavier; but he was able to carry it all alone. Then I took the top of a Russian thistle plant and put it on the hill. The ants looked it over and tried to move it. But it was too large, even for their combined strength. So they set to work, cutting the leaves with their powerful jaws and carrying away the pieces. Finally they were able to move what was left, and they carried that away.

I noticed two ants coming out of the runway. One was backing out pulling something after it, and the other was underneath pushing. When they came out on top I saw that their burden was a stone several times as large as both the ants together. When one looks at one of those anthills, and then around at all the other hills dotting the prairies, one realizes that ants do a tremendous amount of work.

How strong is an ant? I don't know exactly. Someone has estimated that if a man were as strong as an ant in proportion to his size, he could lift one hundred and twenty tons, or about 1,350 times his own weight.

Why are ants so strong? If you take time to watch them at work, you will soon see the reason. They have to dig the hard earth, they have to lift and carry stones and sticks and all sorts of things. They have to be strong in order to do their work, to live their lives. When you examine an ant you wonder wherein his strength lies. He is sparely built. Surely those legs, as thin as a fine thread, can have no great strength; but they have. The head of an ant is a very tower of strength, with its powerful mandibles, or jaws, for cutting and grasping.

The ant teaches us a great deal about how carefully God has fitted his creatures to do their work, each in its own way. The author of Proverbs (6:6) said, "Go to the ant, thou sluggard; consider her ways, and be wise." When we study the ant, we can see the fingerprints of God, the marks of his handiwork, the signs that God is not unmindful of these little things. And we can be sure that he is not unmindful of us.

William M. Orr

75 *A LESSON FROM THE BIRDS*

Two small boys, who lived in an English town near the famous White Cliffs of Dover, went out one spring day to collect some birds' eggs. Looking up a tall cliff they spied a nest. They felt certain that they could reach the nest, if they were very careful. So up to the top of the cliff they went. One boy leaned over as far as possible, and the other held firmly to his legs.

It was fortunate for them that the owner of the nest was away from home! For the nest belonged to a peregrine falcon. They are fierce birds of prey.

What do you think the small English boys found in the nest? Eggs, of course. But they also found something more. They found three little tubes attached to what had been the legs of carrier pigeons. In the tubes they found messages. The boys took the tubes to the town constable. He realized that these

A Lesson from the Birds

messages were from airmen and that they had been addressed to the Royal Air Force.

How did those messages get into that falcon's nest? Perhaps you can guess. The Royal Air Force knew. Let me tell you about one of the messages.

Early one morning a bomber of the Royal Air Force had completed its "mission," found its target, and then turned home again. As the great plane was crossing the English Channel, an enemy plane appeared. There was a blaze of fire and the Royal Air Force plane was hit. The plane crashed into the water. The flyers were saved because their life raft provided a little tossing island for them.

Almost immediately they wrote a message to inform the rescue crews of their location. The message was put in a tube and the tube was attached to the pigeon they always carried with them. Away that faithful bird flew toward England and help.

High up in the air another bird, a peregrine falcon, soared and hovered. Seeing this pigeon far below, the falcon hurtled itself through the air, pounced upon the hapless pigeon, and took it back to its own nest.

Think of all that the pigeon's flight meant. Young men tossing upon the rough waters were in danger. Mothers and fathers back home were anxious for their sons' safety. If only that falcon had known that the pigeon was a "fellow bird" and that excitement and food can be obtained in less harmful ways!

But we don't expect birds to think that way. Yet you and I can understand what no bird can know. We can understand that all human life is precious to friends and family and to God. Sometimes we forget that we are all God's children and belong to the same human family. We must think and pray and act as though we belonged to God's human family. We cannot, like the falcon, destroy each other and still hope to have a peaceful, happy world, the kind of world Christ died to make.

David A. MacLennan

76 *LIVING TO SERVE*

There is something gloriously unselfish about a brook. Unlike a lake, which gathers to itself and for itself streams and runoff waters from adjacent hills, a brook lives to serve, not to be served, to give, not to receive. It gathers ground water and springs to itself but not for itself, only to offer them again to the larger streams and the lakes and the seas. Wherever it goes, among the joyfully uplifted hills or the sad and somber swamps, the brook exists to spend itself and to be spent, giving its waters freely, asking nothing in return.

One might almost think that it is this unselfish character of the brook that makes it such a happy thing. It lopes laughingly through low-lying swamps, by the side of a deeply rutted road, then through a culvert and out among groves of cedars and past delicate birches. It dashes gleefully under fences, past the spire-like sentinels of balsam and spruce and the miscellany of poplar, black ash, beech and maple. Other companionable little creeks join the brook as it skips and runs toward the patiently waiting lake.

A brook is going somewhere. It is water-on-a-mission. About to present itself to other waters at its destination, it never neglects little wayside opportunities. On its way to make its final offering, it gaily gives itself all along the way. Deer drink of its refreshing coolness with a deep content. Boys of seven years and of seventy probe its pools and eddies with their lures and return home at day's end with the brook's gift of speckled trout. Fish, crustaceans, mollusks, and water insects are given a home in its swirling currents and tranquil pools. From its birth in bubbling springs to its arrival at its final goal the brook is selfless and a happy-appearing thing.

Service and happiness belong together. We feel lowest when we are most self-centered, when we are most self-pitying. We are happiest when we are so busy doing for others that we forget ourselves.

A person's circumstances may be ever so favorable, but he will be unhappy if he is self-centered. His troubles may be many, but he may still achieve happiness if he lives by the service motive. In the shadow of the cross, on the eve of his crucifixion, the Master said to his disciples, "These things have I spoken unto you, that my joy might remain in you, and that your joy might be full" (John 15:11). His joy? What reason did he have to be joyful with suffering confronting him on the morrow? Christ's joyousness came from giving himself for others.

Like the brook, we are here not to get, but to give.*

Harold E. Kohn

77 THE FISH THAT IS A STAR

These see . . . his wonders in the deep. PSALM 107:24

Here we have today one of the wonders of the deep. It is a fish that looks like a star. Down at the seashore you can find them at the end of a jetty or on the beach when the tide is out. I know there is a great difference between this little fish and the beautiful stars we see in the heavens at night. Yet God made this poor creature in the form of a beautiful star! It reminds me of a little verse by Ralph Waldo Emerson that goes:

> But in the mud and scum of things
> There alway, alway something sings.

Amid the mud of lakes and rivers, and amid the sand and rocks of the oceans, God has put "his wonders in the deep." I wonder if any boy or girl here today has ever looked through a microscope. I remember once looking through a microscope at some mud from the bottom of a river. To my surprise, I saw many curious and beautiful creatures. Some of them looked like little wheels and each of them kept revolving round and round as if his very life depended on not stopping. They were called by some big name that I couldn't pronounce. So it is with all of nature. The snowflake, the pollen of the flower, the blade of grass put under a microscope are all beautiful beyond anything we can imagine. God made them that way.

Once upon a time a scientist was making a study of the heather bell, the little blue flower that blooms so sweetly on the hills of Scotland. He was examining the spray when a great, burly Scotch shepherd came by and stopped to see what the scientist was doing. The scientist said nothing, but simply beckoned to the shepherd to look through the microscope. As the old man looked, tears began to run down his weather-beaten cheeks. Handing the instrument back, the big Scotsman said, "To think this great foot o' mine has trod on so many o' them!" The beauty that God had put into that tiny flower made him ashamed that he had not appreciated it before, ashamed that he had stepped on it.

So we trample on so much of the beauty that God has made

and never think about it. Or we pass by such a fish as this without noticing that it really is shaped like a star, and that a star is a beautiful thing.

This starfish teaches us also that we, too, can be like the stars. . . . The Bible tells us that "they that are wise shall shine . . . as the stars for ever and ever" (Dan. 12:3). By "wise" it means those that follow Jesus and try to win others to him here in the world.

The smallest of us, the weakest and plainest of us here on earth, can be beautiful. We can someday "shine like the stars." That ought to teach us to be faithful, and to do the best we know how for God in the place where he has put us.*

E. Lansing Bennett

78   THE HERALD OF THE GREAT KING

Yesterday Francis had been one of the richest young men in the whole city of Assisi, Italy. Today he had not a penny in the world, and no better garment than a rough homespun tunic given him by a farm servant. But Francis was not pitying himself. He was striding through the woods, singing at the top of his voice. And a very good voice it was, too.

Francis had made his own decision to give up what men call riches so that he could give all his attention to being "rich toward God." He was free now of all the selfish problems that wealth brings. He had gone out into the woods alone to talk with God about his new way of living.

Never before had the woods looked half so beautiful to Francis. The sun, filtering down through the trees, made him think of the warmth and brightness of God's love. The clear brooks, splashing their way to the rivers, seemed to be singing of the refreshing purity of God's way. The wind, rushing through the treetops blowing the clouds across the sky, and brushing his cheek, seemed to tell of both God's strength and God's gentleness. All the tiny creatures of the woodland—birds, squirrels, insects—seemed to be joining in a glad song of praise to God. All nature seemed to be singing, "God made us! Let us praise him!"

Francis joined in the song. He had always had a good voice, though he had used it before in singing ballads to entertain friends at parties. Now a new kind of song rolled from his lips, a song in praise of the God who made the world so beautiful and so friendly. Not knowing what was hiding behind a pile of rocks, Francis walked on, the happiest young man in all Assisi.

"Who are you?" It was the harsh voices of robbers who were irritated at hearing anyone so happy. They stood in front of Francis, glaring at him and blocking his path. "Who are you?"

A few days ago Francis would have answered haughtily, "I am Francis, son of Pietro Bernadone, the merchant of Assisi."

But the answer that Francis gave instead was so different that it surprised even him. "I am a herald of the Great King."

Even the robbers knew, from the voice in which Francis described himself as a herald of the Great King, that he meant that he was a herald of God. This made them even more angry than his singing had done. They grabbed him by his homespun tunic, shook him roughly, and threw him into a ditch.

"Lie there!" they shouted. "Lie there, lout! You herald of the Great King!"

But it took more than that to stop Francis' singing. Not only during that day and during the days when he was a young man was Francis the herald of the Great King. The longer he lived in the world God made, the more beautifully did the sun, the moon, the stars, the animals, the birds, the flowers, the fire, the wind, and the water speak to him of God's goodness. Best of all animals he loved the lambs, whose gentleness reminded him of God's gentleness. Best of all birds he loved the larks, whose way of soaring skyward as they sang made him sure it was the praises of God they were singing. Fire seemed such a precious gift from God that Francis hated to put out a spark or blow out a candle. Francis called all bits of God's world his brothers and his sisters. He would sing songs to Brother Sun and Sister Moon, to Brother Wind and Sister Water. All through his life the rich voice of the herald of the Great King joined with the voices of nature in praising the Creator of all things.

Finally the time came when Francis was old and sick and almost blind. Kind friends had built him a little hut of reeds where he could lie in the garden and enjoy the songs of the birds, the fragrance of the flowers, the humming of the wind, the warmth of the sunshine. It would seem that Francis' days as herald of the Great King were ended.

But, fortunately for us, he had one more song to give. He called his friends about him and sang, in a voice that was still sweet though it was no longer strong, his last song—the "Hymn of the Sun."

He taught it to his friends so that they could sing it to him as he lay dying. Seven centuries have gone by since then, but we still sing Francis' "Hymn of the Sun." We can find it with music in some hymnbooks, with the title "All Creatures of Our God and King."

Alice Geer Kelsey

165

Something is taking place in the meadows and woods, on mountain ranges and in the depths of the sea, that will also be happening to you today. Cows, sheep, horses, goats, birds, insects, fish, and all other creatures are eating so that they can stay alive, just as you will eat dinner today when you get home from church. The pastures are dotted with animals grazing in grass and browsing on shrubs, calves devouring grass so that they might become cows, colts feeding so that they might grow into horses, and lambs munching on grass blades so that they might become sheep. And, of course, little pigs are stuffing themselves with corn, making hogs of themselves!

Mountain goats and mountain sheep seek out tender shoots of grass and leaves of shrubs among the rocks. Birds while in flight catch insects and they also search for insects in rotting logs or they pick seeds from flowers. Insects feed on other insects or on plant juices and on a multitude of other things. Fishes in streams and lakes and seas eat other fishes or tiny swimming animals and floating plants. And around the family dinner table today most of you will pause for grace and then say, "Please pass the potatoes!"

All this eating, which absorbs so much of our interest and our time, amounts to one thing. Creatures are moving the good things from outside of them to the inside of them. It is the only way they can stay alive and be strong. Drinking and breathing are other ways in which by absorbing a part of our surroundings we draw the outside inside of us.

No living thing is self-sufficient. Everything that stays alive depends upon finding the good that is outside of it, and welcoming it inside. We do that with food, with fresh, sparkling water, and with good clean air, whenever we eat or drink or breathe.

The mind, like the body, is kept alive, healthy and growing by inviting the good things inside. An eye is a doorway through which the good comes. It should always be open to the beauty of sunrises and sunsets, distant stars and smiling faces. It should be open, too, to inspiring reading such as we find in the Holy Bible and in the stories of great leaders of the race. The ear is another door that should stand open to the best we can find in our surroundings. Through the ear come the advice of older and wiser people than ourselves, the instruction of teachers, the preaching of the gospel, and the sound of music which stirs and inspires us. Our senses are ways by which outside effects are felt within.

Worship, fellowship with friends, play, and all your happiest experiences are ways by which you gladly receive outside influences into your mind. And you mentally chew upon them and digest them until they become a part of you, making you a bigger and better person.

But something ought to be said, too, about the bad things around us that we don't want inside. What are we to do about them? Here is some good news! We are created with the equipment to keep the worst influences outside where they belong. That is the reason you have eyelashes. Your eyes let in the good, but the eyelashes are meant for keeping out the dirt. Their purpose is to keep foreign matter like insects and dust away from our delicate and easily hurt eyes. Our mouths do not stand idly open. We have lips that open for food, but they can be closed, too, against blowing dirt or sand. So you have, even now, a sense of right and wrong that works like eyelids and like shut lips, barring the undesirable from your mind. The worst doesn't have to get in. You can know that cheating exists in your surroundings without letting cheating become a part of you. You may never, in this life, be able to escape the presence of lies or swearing or other evils around you. They may be present nearby. But your well-trained sense of right and wrong will keep them outside of you, so that they will never become a part of you.

The surest way, then, to grow from what we are to what we want to be is to bring the best things of life from the outside inside and to leave the wrong standing outside, uninvited. The Apostle Paul put it this way: "Whatever is true, whatever is honorable, whatever is just, whatever is pure, whatever is lovely, whatever is gracious, if there is any excellence, if there is anything worthy of praise, think about these things" (Phil. 4:8, RSV). That is how the soul stays alive.

Harold E. Kohn

11. TALKING WITH GOD

80 THE BOY WHO NEVER SPOKE TO HIS FATHER

Did you ever hear of *The Boy Who Never Spoke to His Father?* No? Well, let me tell you about him.

The father provided everything for his boy, a house to live in, clothes to wear, food to eat, toys to play with, everything that heart could wish; but he never once said, "Thank you, Father."

The father was wonderfully kind and loving, strong and good, gentle toward the weak, thoughtful for all, and again and again had shown his tenderness and love to this boy, but never did he say, "Father, I love you."

The boy was often disobedient and rebellious and brought shame and reproach on his father, but never did he say, "Father, forgive me."

The father was wise, and always ready to help, to teach, to guide; but never did the boy say, "Father, show me the way!"

And the boy had brothers, some of whom did not seem to have as many of the good things of life as he had; but this boy never seemed to care; at any rate, he never asked his father to help his brothers.

There was never such a boy? Oh, yes, there are many of them, I fear. Every boy who does not pray is *The Boy Who Never Spoke to His Father.*

"When ye pray, say 'Our Father—'"

Avery Albert Shaw

81   *OUR LINK TO GOD*

There is a Danish fable about a spider which built his web in a barn. He began high up among the rafters, where he started to spin a long, thin thread, and attached the end of it to one of the beams. Then he jumped off, not in the least afraid, for although the thread was very thin, he knew that it was tough enough to bear his weight, and that the beam above was very strong. Spinning out more thread, he continued to descend.

Having reached the spot where the center of the web was to be, he sent out other threads like the spokes of a wheel, fixing them to the walls and other suitable holding places. Next, beginning at the center, he spun another thread in a spiral fashion—round and round, the circles becoming bigger as he went—and fastened it at each point where it crossed the "spokes."

By this time he had the necessary framework of the right size and shape. But his task wasn't finished yet. He began again at the outside with a different kind of thread—a sticky thread this time, going round and round in smaller and smaller circles until he reached the center. Then the web was complete, and he was very proud of it. "Now I'll catch many flies," he said, "and have plenty of food." This he did, and he soon grew fat and was very pleased with himself.

One day, however, as he wandered about his web, he saw the long, fine thread stretching upward toward the roof. "I wonder what that's for?" he said. "It doesn't catch any flies. Why did I ever put it away up there?" And so, thinking it of no use, he broke it. Then a sad thing happened, for no sooner had he broken it than all his wonderful web collapsed.

How foolish of the spider to forget the purpose of that thread, on which everything depended. How foolish to break the line that linked him with the strong, supporting beam above. And wouldn't you or I be just as foolish if we forgot our need of prayer, and broke the link by which we take hold of the strength of God?

H. W. Hitchcock

82   THREE BOYS AND A DOG

Three boys and a dog clambered up a rocky slope near the Sea of Galilee. The boys hesitated as the path forked, one branch going along a level ridge and the other branch going steeply up among sharp rocks and scraggling bushes. But the dog knew where to go. With a wag of his shaggy tail, he bounded up the steeper path.

"The dog is right." Jonathan pointed at fresh sandal prints in the dust of the harder trail. "He took the steep path."

Up the hillside after the dog scrambled the boys. It was hard going, but not too hard for boys who at least saw within reach something they had long desired, the chance to have some time alone with Jesus. He was such good company for boys, but what use was it to have him for their best friend when he was always surrounded by crowds of grownups? He knew the answers to all the boys' questions. Better still, he could show them how to find out the answers to their own questions. But what was the use? The minute they had him to themselves, somebody big and important was sure to come along and interrupt.

"No fat rabbis or dressed-up Pharisees will trail him up this path!" Ezra picked himself up, puffing and rubbing his bruised knee.

"Perhaps he can finish the story he started to tell us yesterday while he was whittling a doll for little Ruth," said Simeon. "Was I disgusted when that beggar woman came up with her sobbing story! I know he would rather talk with us than listen to her."

Nearing the top of the hill, the boys saw their friend standing, head high and arms outstretched. They let out a yell of recognition, but Jesus did not turn.

"Funny he does not hear us." Jonathan put his hands to his mouth and called again. Still Jesus did not seem to hear.

The boys climbed nearer.

Now he was walking slowly back and forth.

Jonathan took a deep breath, preparing for another loud call. Suddenly Ezra clapped his hand over Jonathan's mouth.

"Sh!" whispered Ezra. "Look at Jesus' face."

The boys gazed in wonder at the face of their friend. It always shone with kindness and understanding. Now there was something even bigger there.

"He seems to be talking with someone who makes him very, very happy." Simeon's voice was full of awe. "Yet he is alone!"

"No, not alone," said Jonathan slowly. "God is on that hilltop with Jesus."

"He calls God his Father," said Ezra reverently, "and now I see what he means. God is so close to him that he can talk to God as easily as we talk to our fathers and mothers."

The boys sat down on the hillside, all thought of interrupting Jesus gone. They would wait. In silence, they watched Jesus, alone with God. Gradually they came to find a new meaning of what prayer meant, of what worship meant. Gradually there came to them a new understanding of Jesus' strength. He could do wonderful things because he let God's strength flow into him. He was full of joy because he truly loved and worshiped the Maker of all.

The setting sun touched the hilltop. The boys looked longingly at their friend, who had not once sensed their presence. They hated to leave without talking to him, but they respected his praying. The little dog wagged his tail understandingly when the boys ordered him to stand on guard while they went down the hill to their supper and their beds.

Early after sunrise the next morning the boys hurried up the mountain trail again. Soon their little dog bounded out to meet them. They heard strong, steady footsteps and a clear joyous voice raised in song. Around a curve in the trail came Jesus, his face alight with a gladness and a power beyond all imagining.

The boys slipped into step at his side for the climb down the hillside. There was no need of asking where he had been or what he had been doing. They knew that he had been with God.

Alice Geer Kelsey

83   THE LITTLE THAT IS MUCH

What are they among so many? JOHN 6:9

That is what Andrew said to Jesus as he looked at the little fellow's loaves and fishes, and then at the hungry multitude. How could you divide five small cakes and two small fishes to feed five thousand people? Why, there was only a single meal in the lot. How on earth could you cut them up into five thousand parts? Each person would have required a microscope to see his helping, and even then the particle might be lost before reaching the mouth. No, it couldn't be done. Andrew was right, and yet he was wrong. If he had just said, "Master, a boy here has a morsel of fish and bread, but I believe you can make that go round the whole crowd." Had he said that, it would have shown the depth of his faith, and it was purposely to test the depth of his faith that Jesus asked how much would be required to give every man, woman and child a meal. Andrew, who had seen Jesus work miracles, didn't think, at that moment, that even a miracle was fit to feed that great crowd of people. In the boy's basket were only five little cakes and two small fishes, but in Christ's hands they multiplied to an enormous degree.

Aren't some of us like Andrew? We think things are not worth much, and therefore we do not give them. Of such things we say, "What are these? They are no good to anyone. I'd rather give nothing than give these."

The lad had but little in his basket, yet that little in the hands of Christ increased more than five-thousandfold.

Boys and girls, you simply cannot tell the exact value of what you give. It was only ten cents a little girl paid for her father's birthday gift. He did not need cuff links. He had a beautiful gold pair, and this was only a ten-cent pair. That is true, but when they were lovingly placed in his hand by his own little girl, they mounted up in value. Indeed, he placed his own gold ones in a drawer, and wore the brass ones. They were worth only ten cents as they lay in the shop, but when they passed into his hands they were beyond price, for they were plated with the love of a little girl.

Now I wonder if you have any little gifts you can offer to God? You don't think much of your little prayers sometimes.

What are they among so many big prayers that are going up to God?

"I want to speak to God," said a little girl, "but I know he won't hear me. Will you speak for me, Daddy?" And what did the father tell her? He said, "If God were surrounded by the angels of heaven, who were singing their sweetest song to him, he would say, 'Hush, my angels, there is a little girl away down on the earth who has something to say to me, and I want to hear her.' "

Don't think your prayers are not heard, for God values them. And he values your kind words, and your little deeds of love. You may say of them, "What are these?" But little as they seem, they are precious in the eyes and ears of God, and he makes them go further than ever you could imagine.*

J. Lyle Rodger

84   PRAYERS THAT GOD DOES NOT ANSWER

Ye ask, and receive not, because ye ask amiss. JAMES 4:3

God does not always give us what we ask in our prayers. If he did, it would not be well for us.

There was a young man in prison for committing a great crime. I met an old man who had known that young man all his life. He said: "The trouble with that boy was that his father spoiled him. He gave him everything that he wanted. If the father had been a little wiser, the boy would not have been ruined."

Your fathers and mothers do not give you everything that you ask for. If they did, it would be a bad thing for you. And God deals in the same way with us. If he were to grant us everything that we ask, it would harm instead of help us.

Very often we ask him to do something for us that we ought to do for ourselves. When I was in school once in a while one of the boys would come to a problem that was very hard. After looking at it for a moment he would take it to his teacher and ask him to work it for him. The teacher would say to him, "Now, my boy, it is not going to do you any good if I work this problem. You go back and see if you can solve it yourself."

That boy had been sent to school that his mind might grow strong by working hard problems and doing hard things. So his teacher did not do what he asked, but made him work it out for himself. He wanted his teacher to do something for him that he ought to have done for himself.

If you ever pray to God asking him to do something for you and he does not do it, ask yourself if it is not a problem that he wants you to work out for yourself. We ought never to trouble God with things that we can do for ourselves.

Then sometimes boys and girls pray for clear weather. They are going on an excursion, perhaps, the next day, and they are afraid that it will rain, so they ask God to give them a clear, bright day. The next morning when they wake up the first sound they hear is the rain coming down on the roof. They are disappointed, and they think that God has not heard their prayer. But God has a very large family to take care of, and he has to think about all his people. Out in the country there are thousands of farmers who have planted their fields and they are praying for rain to come and make the crops grow. If God were to answer your prayer and send sunshine every day, there would be no rain and the farmers would have no fruit or grain, and there would be nothing to eat. God has to think of all his children, and if he sends you rain when you ask for sunshine, just think of all the blessings that the rain brings to the earth, the grain, the fruit and the flowers.

I read once of a fairy who was asked by the people to pray to God for rain. Before she prayed, she thought she would find out what day would be the most convenient for the people to have it rain. Well, the women did not want it to rain on Monday, for that was washday, and Tuesday the market people wanted clear weather. Wednesday the farmers were going to cut their hay and Thursday they were planning to gather it in; Friday and Saturday it was something else, and, of course, the ministers did not want it to rain on Sunday. There was no day that suited everyone. So the fairy went and asked the Lord to send the rain whenever he thought best, and that is the way he sends it.

Sometimes we are very selfish in our prayers. There was a boy who wanted a quarter very much to buy something that he needed, and he had no way of getting it, so he prayed that he might find a quarter. That seems like a harmless prayer, but it isn't so harmless as we think. If he were to find a quarter someone else would have first to lose it.

He was asking God to take the money out of the pocket of someone else and put it into his. We must be sure that our prayers, if they are granted, do not make someone else suffer. If they do, God may not answer them.

We will all pray many times when God does not answer, and the reason is not that he does not hear us, but that we are asking for something that is not right, or is not best.

Stuart Nye Hutchison

12. GOD'S HOUSE

❧

BE THANKFUL

When you go riding in the family car, where do you usually sit? In the back? Or up front with the driver? Most boys and girls like the front seat where there is so much to see and where they can make believe they are driving the car.

A boy I know was going to church school with his mother, father and sister. Naturally he ran out and sat in the front seat. But it wasn't his turn, and when he was told to sit in the back, he started to whimper and complain. In fact he became so angry that he said he wouldn't go to church unless he could sit up front. His sister, who was a little older, was surprised to hear this. "Imagine not going to God's House," she said, "just because you can't ride in the front seat."

I am sure you would have felt the same way. Just think, not wanting to go to God's House because he couldn't sit where he wanted! But it might be surprising to you also to know that there are a number of people who make similar excuses. They say they won't go to God's House because they don't have a new dress, or because they don't like the minister or church-school teacher, because the seats are not comfortable enough, because the church is too crowded, too cold or too hot.

Centuries ago a very devout person told how he went to God's House: "I went with the throng, and led them in procession to

the house of God, with glad shouts and songs of thanksgiving"
(Psalm 42:4, RSV). And David wrote: "I was glad when they said
to me, 'Let us go to the house of the Lord!' " (Psalm 122:1, RSV).

If we go to God's House with joy in our hearts and if we are
thankful to God for his many blessings, then it won't much
matter where we ride or what we wear. We will be too grateful
to have selfishness in our hearts or excuses on our lips.

John Schott

86   *ONE REASON WHY WE GO TO CHURCH*

How many of you have your own rooms in your houses? And
what do you have in those rooms? Do you have your own pictures, ones which you have chosen yourselves? And do you have
there a place to keep your special treasures, shells, stones,
stamps, coins, or butterflies which you have collected yourself?
Perhaps you also have some things of which you were once very
fond, but which now look to you rather childish and foolish.
Here, for instance, is a stick which does not mean anything at all
to anyone else. But it does mean a great deal to you, for you
found it the day you went on a mountain hike with your Scout
Troop. Every time you look at it, you think of the good time
you had that day. Probably all of us, children and older people
too, have in our rooms things which we like, not because of
their usefulness, but because they make us think of happy times,
or of friends whom we love very much. Like mirrors, they reflect
pleasant experiences and close companions. We like to touch
them, to look at them now and then, because it is fun to recall
those days and friends.

Things which you can see or touch and that make you think

at the same time of things that you cannot see and touch are what we call symbols.

When you go to church, you see there a number of things which make you think of things which you cannot see. Perhaps there are two vases on the altar or communion table, and when you look at them, perhaps you think of the person in whose memory they were given. They are a symbol of him. The flowers in the vases are a symbol of the beauty of nature. Perhaps there is a Cross in your church. That is only a piece of wood or metal. But it is also a great symbol—the symbol of Christianity. It makes us think of Jesus of Nazareth, who was loyal and faithful even unto death, and of the thousands and thousands of people who have suffered for what they believed to be right.

The collection plates are also symbols, because they are a reminder of how fortunate we are to be able to give each Sunday an expression of gratitude for all that we have received and enjoy as members of the great family of God to which we all belong.

But more than all these, does not the church itself make you think of the things that mean the most to you, when you are at your best? It makes you think of your love for your family and friends, your hopes for your school and home life, your dreams of the kind of person you want to be, and more than anything else, of your relationship to God. In other words, the church itself is a symbol of the best that is in us all. And this is one of the very greatest reasons for going to church—for it does us good to be reminded by the symbols about which I have been telling you, the symbols of all the beautiful things in life which can neither be seen nor touched.

Dan Huntington Fenn

87   *WHEN ERIC CHOSE TO HELP*

Eric was walking proudly down the street beside his tall father. He was not holding on to his father's hand, because an almost-six-year-old boy was too big to do that any more, he thought; but it *was* rather hard to keep up with his father's big steps unless he did, or unless he skipped every now and then. That is what Eric was doing today. Three big steps and the two skips kept him beside his father without much trouble. That is, it did until David and Jamie called to him. Then, because his father was in a hurry, and because it was rude not to answer, Eric had to run to catch up again. He was all out of breath when his father asked him what the boys had wanted.

"They are going to the lot to rake leaves and play in them, and they wanted me to go."

"And didn't you want to go?" asked Father.

"No; I can play in the leaves any day, but I can't always go with you to the church. I told them that, and they said—" But there Eric stopped. He did not like to tell what they had said.

"What did they say?" asked Father, slowing up a bit so that Eric need not be quite so much out of breath.

Eric's face was very red, as he replied: "They said that my father is only a janitor, anyway. But I don't feel that way, Father," and Eric forgot he was almost six, and slipped his hand into his father's large one. "Besides, I think that taking care of God's House is the very best job any father could have. They don't know how nice it is inside the church. I like it, though I like it best on Sunday mornings."

Eric's father smiled, and pressed the hand in his. "You have reason to feel that way, Son," he said, "though it does not make any difference when we go into God's House. We can always remember him, whether we are working, or whether we are worshiping. But today I am going to let you help."

Eric's eyes shone. "That's what little Samuel did," he said. "I learned that in Sunday school, how he helped around the church."

"And so can you sometimes. Here we are now," and the key slipped into the lock as soon as the words were spoken. Then the door swung open and they found themselves in the big hall, with the stairs opening into it. Eric stood still while his father went for the dusters, and then they went up the stairs together. Into the big auditorium they went, where all seemed hushed and still. Eric loved this stillness. He wondered whether the boy Samuel had felt that way about his church.

"We will dust down the big long pews first," said Father. "We must do them carefully, so the people who come tomorrow to worship in God's House will not get dust on their clothes."

Eric carefully dusted the shiny cushioned seats, and the smooth wooden backs of the pews, one by one. When they were finished they shone in the sunlight that streamed in through the beautiful windows. The sunshine always seemed brighter when it came through those windows. Eric liked to think it was because of the pictures on them, the picture of Jesus and the little children, and of the baby Jesus himself, and others.

"Now," said Father, "we must dust the organ, Eric. But be very careful."

Eric *was* careful. He had not known there were so many parts to an organ; the rows of shining keys, the many foot pedals—which Father said help to make the music—and all the carved pieces in the wood.

"They make the things in a church nice and beautiful, don't

they, Father?" Eric almost whispered.

"Yes, indeed. That is one way we have of showing that we want to worship God. People give money so that others may have a beautiful place to worship in. It makes folks want to give thanks. It makes them think of the Heavenly Father. Come here, Eric, where you can see the beautiful windows better. See how the light shines through? Is it any wonder people want to worship God in here?"

"It makes me feel that way, too, Father. Oh, I'm so glad that this is God's House, and that I can help you keep it clean!"

On Sunday morning, a very happy little boy sat beside his mother in church. Everything was clean and shining. He had helped to make it so. As the heads were bowed in prayer, Eric added a little one of his own: "Thank you, Heavenly Father, for your house—and for letting me help—I will take care of it always."

Mary C. Odell

88   *THE BUSY-AS-A-BEAVER CHURCH*

"He's as busy as a beaver." You have all heard people say that, and that remark has real meaning because the beaver is an intelligent, hard-working, ambitious animal. Will you believe that beavers have been known to build dams that are a thousand feet long? And in addition to building dams, each pair of beavers gathers food for winter and builds its own two-story home. So when someone says of you, "You're busy as a beaver," that's quite a compliment.

But do you know that God has given the beaver a good reason for keeping busy? It isn't simply the need to gather food, or to build homes and dams, that keeps the beaver a busy animal.

The beaver cuts down trees with four sharp front teeth called incisors. With these chisellike teeth he can cut through trees as thick as two feet. But the strange thing about these teeth is that they never stop growing. When a beaver wears away his teeth by gnawing through wood, the teeth grow again. If the beaver stops using his chisellike teeth for very long they grow to such a length that he cannot even open and shut his mouth to eat. So, if a beaver doesn't work he doesn't eat.

And that applies to the young beavers, too. For when a colony of beavers builds or repairs a dam, every beaver in the colony, old and young, works. Although occasionally a beaver may live alone, most beavers prefer to live in families or colonies.

Now you are beginning to see why a church ought to be a busy-as-a-beaver church. In the church all members, old and young, ought to work together for the good of all. This ought to be true in families, communities, schools, and factories, too. But above all, in the church we should be as busy as beavers and try to make the church more beautiful, pleasant, and helpful.

The Apostle Paul thought that every Christian should work hard. When writing to the Thessalonians he said, "For even when we were with you, we gave you this command: If any one will not work, let him not eat" (2 Thess. 3:10, RSV). He knew that nothing great and good could be accomplished unless everyone did his share.

In the church we work and worship together as the family of God. When we worship in the Lord's House, we sit down at the Lord's Table. We do not feast on meat and potatoes, peaches and ice cream, but we feast on truth, music, mercy, beauty, and love. These feed our souls. God provides us the bread of life through his Word. And we enjoy this feast that gives strength to our souls.

Someone has to work along with God to supply all the good things that come to us through the church. The pastor, organist, choir director, teachers, custodian, superintendents, officers, and ushers have to be as busy as beavers. But with all they do, there is work still left for each of you. You, too, must be busy as a beaver.

Galen E. Hershey

89   *HUMPTY DUMPTY GOES TO CHURCH*

A young man named Eutychus was sitting in the window. He sank into a deep sleep as Paul talked still longer; and being overcome by sleep, he fell down from the third story and was taken up dead. But Paul went down and bent over him, and embracing him said, "Do not be alarmed, for his life is in him."   ACTS 20:9-10 (RSV)

Do you remember the sad story of Humpty Dumpty?

> Humpty Dumpty sat on a wall,
> Humpty Dumpty had a great fall,
> All the King's horses,
> And all the King's men,
> Couldn't put Humpty Dumpty together again.

Who was Humpty Dumpty? He was an egg. When you first heard that nursery rhyme, how did you picture Humpty Dumpty? Wasn't he a saucy little fellow, who grinned down at you from the top of a wall over which his legs dangled? I remember a picture of him in which he had a smirk on his face. His eyes were shut, and I am sure that is why he fell from the wall.

We have to be careful with Humpty Dumpty. We must not

let him sit on a wall. Not all the king's horses nor all the king's men could put him together again after he had fallen from his perch.

Sometimes there are boys and girls, and men and women too, who make us think of Humpty Dumpty. This is not because they look like an egg, roly-poly and all that, but because they don't keep awake when they should. They may be too tired on Sunday morning to go to church and give our Heavenly Father their love and receive from him the love he offers when we worship him.

In the Bible there is a story of a boy, named Eutychus, who was like Humpty Dumpty. When he got to church, he found that all the seats were taken. So he climbed up and sat on a window ledge. The preacher that day was a great orator named Paul. He had much to say in his sermon. As he talked, the young fellow got drowsier and drowsier. At last he went to sleep. He swayed back and forth until at last he fell from the ledge and onto the courtyard below. The people feared that Eutychus could not be helped. But St. Paul knew a Great Doctor and he prayed for help. Soon the lad was all right again.

You and I are like Humpty Dumpty, and like Eutychus too, because in spite of all our boasting and all our strength, we are frail. We can get broken. That is why our teachers and parents want us to be careful when we cross busy streets. But we are frail in another way. When we forget about church and Sunday school, we are likely to fall. Many boys and girls have tumbled from high walls because they did not stay on the King's Highway or keep a tight hold of God's hand.

If we are like Humpty Dumpty and Eutychus, can we be lifted up and put together again? In this you and I are different from Humpty Dumpty. Thank goodness! If we fall from a high wall and hurt our souls, we may be forgiven and be given a new life. God gives us a new chance. A friend of mine has added a couple of lines to the nursery rhyme which tells what our Heavenly King can do for us:

> Humpty Dumpty sat on a wall,
> Humpty Dumpty had a great fall,
> Not all the King's horses, nor all the King's men
> Could ever lift Humpty Dumpty again.
> *But along came the King's own precious Son*
> *And gathered the bits and made them one.*
>
> David A. MacLennan

90   *WHAT'S IN A BALLOON?*

And the Lord God . . . breathed into his nostrils the breath of life; and man became a living soul.   GENESIS 2:7

I love colored balloons, don't you? It's such good fun to hit them up into the air, and they look so gay hanging in clusters from the ceiling at parties.

What's in a balloon? Did you say, "Nothing"? Oh, but you are wrong. See, I have brought one with me. I'm going to let out what's inside. There, the balloon is now quite flat, just a bit of crumpled skin. Did you *see* anything come out?

No, you saw nothing; but something did come out because the balloon is now empty. Yes, of course, there was air inside. To be exact, it was breath, my breath. Breath is a word we often use when we talk about spirit. The Bible tells us that when God made man he breathed into him "the breath of life; and man became a living soul."

What's in a Balloon?

What is it that is inside us that makes our bodies living things? It is spirit. Without that spirit this body of ours would be like that empty balloon. Do not think that because you cannot see spirit that there is not such a thing; it is like the breath which as it enters the balloon completely changes it, altering it from a crumpled-up bit of skin into something beautiful and buoyant, something in a way alive, moving with the lightest breath of wind.

I'll blow up this balloon again. Now once again it is full of breath, as full of breath as our bodies are full of spirit. The breath is the breath of man, and the spirit is the spirit of man. But now I want to speak of the Spirit of God, the Holy Spirit.

I have here another balloon. This is blue like the sky, where it seems to want to go. See how it is pulling on this piece of thread and trying to get free. If I let go, it will shoot up to the ceiling. Why? Because it is full of helium, not breath, but helium which is lighter than air. How do I know, for I cannot see anything and it looks no different from the other filled with breath? I know because it rises, and it cannot rise without helium.

Now when the Spirit of God enters a person, he finds himself able to rise to a higher and nobler way of living, to heights of love and goodness. And, too, he finds that he has the power to lift others above the ordinary level of life where people are selfish, ill-tempered, dishonest and all such things, to a higher level altogether, where God's Spirit makes people good and kind, honest and true.

That is what the Spirit of God can do when he enters our lives.

On Pentecost or Whitsunday the Church celebrates the gift of the Holy Spirit as Jesus had promised to his disciples. We read about it in Acts, chapter two, and how from that moment

189

a new power came to the apostles and they themselves became new men, performing many wonders and signs in the name of Jesus Christ.

The gift of the Spirit is meant for all disciples of the Lord Jesus, and it is promised to all. It comes, as it came first of all, when those who love the Lord Jesus meet together for prayer and to share their love of Jesus.

Let us pray in the words of the hymn we often sing:

> Breathe on me, Breath of God;
> Fill me with life anew,
> That I may love what thou dost love,
> And do what thou wouldst do.*

H. Lovering Picken

91   *I KNOW A PATH*

More than two centuries ago a band of nine hundred brave Waldensians, who had been left behind in Switzerland, decided to try to get back to their own homes in Italy. They had been persecuted, starved, hounded from place to place. Often a reward had been offered for those who killed them. They knew great hardships and dangers were to be encountered along the way, but still they wanted to go home.

And the hardships were worse than they had even dreamed. Every day more of their number fell by the way until less than a third of those who had started were able to travel longer. Sometimes they had to fight; sometimes they had to hide; always they had to be hungry, and cold, and fearful.

Finally they came to Mount Cenis, near the border. They had hoped to get across the river and into the security of the mountains without being seen; instead, more than two thousand French troops under Marshal Catenas were drawn up on the other end of the bridge to oppose them.

The Waldensians knew only too well what Marshal Catenas was like. He had defeated the Germans. He had taken Alsace and Lorraine. He had murdered and plundered wherever he went. He was determined that no one should escape. The little band of refugees gathered about their leader hopeless; helpless; seemingly trapped to their death.

"They have ropes ready to hang all who are taken alive," said a soldier. "Better to die by your own hand than to cross the bridge."

"He has waited for you many days. He is angry at the delay," said another soldier. "He will be hard on your women. Turn back! Turn back!"

"What can we do? What shall we do?" cried the brave band of Christians.

"We can pray. We will pray. God is not helpless," said the quiet voice of the one who had taken the place of their old minister, whom they had buried on the hillside in the rear.

As they prayed, one of their number touched the leader on his shoulder, saying,

"Sir! Sir! I know a path! I know a path! I have remembered."

"Tell us of it," whispered the men.

"One day in Italy, when I had lost my goats, I climbed into the high mountains. At night I found a path, I followed it to see where it might lead. It ended, sir, back of us there in the high mountain, not far from Mount Cenis bridge. It is steep. It is very, very dangerous. But it leads home, sir. I know a path that leads home."

"And can you take us to it?" cried the men.

"I can. I will," said the man, eagerly. "I will take you to the path tonight."

So they waited, impatiently, for night to come, hoping to be delivered from their danger. But with the night came the moon—a moon so bright that the night was as the day. All about them the soldiers had built fires, lest the Waldensians try to escape. Again the case seemed hopeless.

"God is not helpless," said the leader again. "We will rest in his care. Pray. Have faith."

Two hours later there was a stir among the Waldensians, for a mist had begun to settle down over the top of the mountain. It was a light mist at first; then it grew denser, until the refugees were hidden from their enemies as carefully as though a wall had been erected between them. Keeping hold of hands, lest they become separated, the Waldensians slowly followed the one of their number who had told of the path.

How could he find it? He had been there but once, and then he had come from Italy, not Switzerland. Yet he marched straight along as though certain of his road. The way seemed endless to the exiles, but in reality they had gone only a little over a mile before they heard their leader saying, "Past this barn. Through a pair of bars. Up a little rise. Ah! Ah!" and he began to sing softly, "Praise God from whom all blessings flow." He had found the path in the mist.

Cliffs rose above them; canyons yawned below. The path had been made slippery by the mist, and it was so narrow that in places it seemed that a man could never walk safely. A single slip of the foot meant certain death. Yet each must walk touching the one ahead, because, in places, the path widened and one might lose his way and his life. Occasionally a loosened stone would go plunging down into the abyss, causing those on the path to shiver with fear. Hour after hour they followed that path until the colors of daybreak were seen in the sky.

At last they came to the entrance of a cave.

"Here you can rest in safety," said the man who had saved them. "Here it is dry, and there are soft leaves for beds. The path at the far end of this cave is in Italy. It is far from our home, but it is in our own beloved land. Thank God, he has shown me the path."

"Aye, we will thank God before we rest," said their spiritual leader. "He has miraculously saved us." So they sat in silence while he recalled to them:

"God is our refuge and strength, a very present help in trouble. . . . Yea, though I walk through the valley of the shadow of death, I will fear no evil: for thou art with me; thy rod and thy staff they comfort me. . . . Bless the Lord, O my soul: and all that is within me, bless his holy Name" (Ps. 46:1; 23:4; 103:1); and kneeling there in the cave, they thanked God for his loving care and guidance.

Margaret W. Eggleston

13. MISSIONARY HEROES

❦

THE MASTER'S VOICE

A nurse in Africa was one day walking along a jungle path, when she heard a strange sound coming from the tall grass nearby. Making her way to the spot, she found a poor, starved African boy, terribly ill. He had been abandoned by the people of his tribe because they believed he had caught the dreaded sleeping sickness and, fearing he might pass it on to others, they had taken him to that lonely spot and left him there to die. The nurse lifted him up, carried him to her home, and then arranged for him to be taken to the mission hospital. The doctor examined him, and found that it wasn't sleeping sickness that had made him ill, but some other trouble that required an operation. As soon as he was strong enough the operation was performed, and after some weeks he was able to return home.

The native folk were greatly impressed by the kindness which had been shown to him. Said one African to another: "Whatever makes the white people take all that trouble over a penniless, starving boy who could pay no fees?"

"They have heard a voice," the other replied, "a voice which says, 'Verily I say unto you, Inasmuch as ye have done it unto one of the least of these my brethren, ye have done it unto me!'" (Matt. 25:40). Yes, the nurse, the doctor, and the other helpers of the mission were giving that splendid service because they, too, had heard and answered the Master's voice.

So with most of the fine things done to help others. They have been done by those who loved to hear his voice, and having heard it, were willing and glad to do the things he asked.*

H. W. Hitchcock

93   WHY DO PEOPLE HAVE FAITH IN US?

Shortly after Robert Moffat went to Africa as a missionary he heard of a savage native chief by the name of Africaner. Africaner was an outlaw. He had been brutally treated by a white farmer of the district in which his tribe lived. The white man had been killed. Africaner became a hunted man with a price of a thousand dollars for his capture. He turned to bloodshed and plunder. Terror of him spread far and wide.

When Robert Moffat heard of the terrible deeds of this savage chieftain he decided to visit him. Some of the white farmers sneered and said that they did not believe he had the courage to make such a trip. Others tried to persuade him not to go, fearing that it would cost him his life. But he was determined. After a journey of great difficulty and hardship he reached the village of Africaner. The chieftain seemed puzzled at the courage of this young missionary, for Robert Moffat was only a little over twenty-one years of age.

Moffat explained to the outlaw that he wanted to live in his village and preach the gospel of Christ's love to his people. Africaner gave his permission and ordered a number of women to build him a hut. Here the young missionary lived for many months, teaching and preaching. He insisted upon providing for his own needs. He often suffered for lack of food. He had to live chiefly on meat and milk. At times he had only milk for three meals a day. Every day he labored to carry on his work. Besides his teaching and preaching there were many other duties to perform. "I am carpenter, smith, cooper, tailor, shoemaker, miller, baker and housekeeper," he wrote in a letter to his parents.

But he carried on. Africaner began to attend his religious services. He learned to read the Bible. He supported Robert Moffat in all of his endeavor to teach the people to be clean in their habits of life and to follow the teachings of Jesus. Soon he too became a Christian.

One day Robert Moffat suggested to Africaner that they go to Cape Town together and that the outlaw give himself up to the authorities. Africaner was amazed. "Why," he said, "I thought you loved me and now you want me to give myself up to the authorities and be hung." But Moffat knew the chieftain could be a completely free man only by following such a course. He urged him to go. Finally, because of his faith in his young missionary friend, Africaner consented. He was willing to put his very life in the hand of a friend he trusted.

Together they went to Cape Town. The humble, intelligent, manly bearing of Africaner made a splendid impression upon all who met him. He was pardoned for his crime and returned to his home with a great shadow of fear and concern removed from his life. After seeing what Christianity had done for such a man, people were more kindly disposed than ever toward the missionary and his work.

Why did Africaner have such faith in Robert Moffat that he would trust him with his life? Because Robert Moffat by his love, his labor, his sacrifice, his unselfish spirit had shown himself to be a true friend. The love of Christ was in his heart and it was continually revealed in all that he was and did. People have faith in us when by our friendly loving, helpful spirit we show ourselves to be worthy of their faith.

Simeon E. Cozad

94 *HIGH CLIMBERS*

I read the story of a little boy a number of years ago who was destined to become a famous man. He was a Scottish lad, who lived in a small kirk town of Scotland a great many years ago, and was very adventurous. He was so adventurous, in fact, that his parents were constantly afraid that some harm would come to him.

Not far from this village was an old and ruined castle. The "keep" or tower was very high, and no one in all the modern years had ever climbed to the top. A fence had been erected about the base of the "keep" so that visitors might not get into danger. But one day this lad climbed to the very top of that "keep," and left his name there on the topmost stone—where, I am told, it may be seen today. When he came down, he was, of course, very properly punished, because his father was afraid that if he kept on in such fashion he would come to an early death.

That boy had courage, but he had more. Presently he had a great purpose, a purpose which became so powerful in his life that it sent him from his village and from his country into the heart of Africa. A few weeks ago in the heart of Africa I saw a waterfall, twice as large as our own Niagara, that this Scottish lad found in the journey that took him clear across the vast continent of Africa. That adventure called for even more courage than the climb to the top of the castle required. Now the boy, grown to manhood, risked his life worthily in a great cause. Indeed, he gave his life because he loved God and was ambitious that the love of God, as we find it in our Lord and Saviour, Jesus Christ, might be revealed to all the men and women and little children of Africa.

The name of the boy who climbed to the top of the old castle tower was David Livingstone, who became the immortal David Livingstone, African explorer, and the intrepid missionary who opened Africa to the Gospel of Jesus Christ.

Daniel A. Poling

95   *THE OPEN DOOR*

When he was a boy he was considered so dull and stupid that it was hardly deemed worth while to keep him in school. No one felt sorry when he left school at fourteen and began to work in a shop where lasts for shoes were made.

Today his name is honored wherever Christian missions are studied, and one of the greatest nations of the world, China, owes him a tremendous debt of gratitude. His name was Robert Morrison.

The change began when he found out a secret: "God and I can do great things." As soon as he began to desire to please God he began to study, even pushing his way through college. In 1804 he was told that he could go to China as the first missionary to that country. So he hired a Chinese student to teach him the language, and he hunted about to get whatever he could to read in Chinese. To his delight, he found in the British Museum a copy of the New Testament in Chinese. This he copied and almost learned. While he was doing it he was beginning his great work for God, though he had no idea that he had really started.

"Do you really think that you can change the great Chinese Empire with all its idol worship and strange beliefs?" asked the man on whose ship he was to sail for China.

"No, indeed," he replied, "but I expect, and know, that God will." In that faith he sailed for the unknown and closed land —in 1807. Having in his possession his copy of the New Testament which he had copied in London, he began to reprint parts of it, hoping in this way to tell the story of Jesus in China. Often his life was in danger; sometimes it seemed to him that his work had been useless; yet for twenty-seven long years he pushed on, believing that God would use what he did to open the doors of China. Then he died and was buried there in China, where he had given his life to the work. He had translated the whole Bible into Chinese, besides publishing a large Chinese dictionary and many other helpful books. This was a tremendous piece of work at that time.

"God has begun to change China," Robert Morrison said at the close of his life, "and I have only helped him a little."

Margaret W. Eggleston

96   *THE SLAVE WHO RETURNED*

Who was St. Patrick? Most folks would say that he was the Irishman who drove the snakes out of Ireland. St. Patrick was a noble Christian, but he was not an Irishman and actually he did not drive snakes out of Ireland. Yet what he did accomplish was far more wonderful.

Patrick was born in Wales more than fifteen centuries ago. When he was a young lad he had a terrible experience. He was captured by rough men and made a slave.

At that time Ireland was inhabited by the wild and savage Scots and Picts. These fierce people got their laborers by raiding the coasts of Britain and Wales. They captured young men and women and took them back as slaves to Ireland. On one of these slave raids, Patrick was captured. After having been held for six long years, he managed to escape. He then traveled in Gaul and through the Mediterranean region before rejoining his family in Wales.

That would make a happy ending for the story, wouldn't it? But it is only the beginning. Patrick resolved to do good to the very people who had wronged him. He would go back to the fierce Irish who had captured him and he would capture them in the name of Christ. Toward the end of his life he recalled why he had made that decision. One night in a dream Christ had spoken to him. "He who laid down his life for you, he it is who speaks to you," Christ said. Patrick awakened with a heart full of joy. Soon he set forth for Ireland, and there he did great work as a Christian missionary. His enthusiastic friends said that when he returned to Ireland there were no Christians and later when his work was completed there were no heathen. He conquered the people in the name of Christ, and made Ireland a Christian land.

How could one man make an impression on such wild and fierce people? There is one universal language which all men of that day understood. That was the language of courage.

Patrick had courage. He stood in the presence of hostile kings and defied them in the name of the King of Kings. More than once attempts were made to kill him. It is said that at one time a friend, who was a chariot driver, learned of secret plans to kill Patrick. The friend urged Patrick to take his place as a driver in a procession. So the driver gave his life that Patrick might be spared.

While living among that race of warriors, Patrick wrote: "Every day I expect either a violent death, or to be defrauded, or to be reduced into slavery, or some such disaster. But none of these things can move me. I trust the promises of heaven. I have cast myself into the hands of Almighty God, for he rules everywhere." And God did care for Patrick and his courage was rewarded. To kings Patrick gave a conscience. To the people he gave a soul. To Ireland he gave Christ and civilization.

Lowell M. Atkinson

14. JESUS, THE CHILDREN'S FRIEND

❧

97   A MILLION MILES TO NOWHERE

Consider him . . . lest ye be wearied.   HEBREWS 12:3

A little paragraph once appeared in a newspaper. It was of no importance. Seemingly it wasn't thought important enough to have a heading in heavy type all to itself; but, for all that, it contained interesting news. It was about an engine driver who had retired after fifty years' service on the railway. He had been given a presentation by his workmates and in thanking them he mentioned that in these fifty years as a driver he had traveled a million miles.

Can you imagine a million miles? It represents nearly one thousand and four hundred return journeys between London and Glasgow. We may think, too, of a million miles representing forty-one journeys, over land and sea, round the world. A journey of a million miles would take us twice to the moon and back with some thousands of miles to spare. Or if the engine driver, on his retirement, had been presented with a penny for every mile he had traveled, he would have received more than £4,000.

Only think of all the places he must have visited and all the sights he must have seen. Think, too, of the great pride he must have taken in the powerful locomotives over which he was in control. Think of the thousands and thousands of people he must have taken on holidays to the seaside and country. He ought to have been very happy in thinking of all the happiness he had given to others in taking them safely to their journey's end. What boy wouldn't be an engine driver when there is all that romance and adventure in the job?

But in imagining all these things about this particular engine driver we would be wrong. Although it is true that in all these years he had traveled a million miles he never once traveled outside of the town in which he lived and worked. He had traveled a million miles to nowhere. Perhaps you don't think that such a thing is possible; but then, you see, he was only a driver on a shunting engine. He had traveled all those million miles up and down a freight yard, banging and clattering trucks and wagons.

Maybe you are saying to yourselves, "What a weary, uninteresting and monotonous job!" But is it really? Certainly this engine driver never had the honor of driving the royal train or the streamlined Royal Scot; he never knew the joy of taking men and women and boys and girls on their holidays. He just shunted about truckloads of coal, pig iron, grain and things of that sort. Yet we mustn't think that because this seems to be a wearisome, uninteresting and monotonous thing to do that it is unimportant. Without the driver of the shunter we would never have heat and light or food and clothing. Not only our health but our very life depends upon men like him doing their work faithfully.

You ought to remember that when you feel, as you sometimes do, that your life is wearisome, uninteresting and monotonous. These are not bad things, for very often they mean dependability. The sun rises every morning; how wearisome! Yes, but how dependable. If it didn't rise one morning we would all be fearful about it. Spring follows winter, summer comes after spring and summer mellows into autumn. How uninteresting, how monotonous! But, again, how dependable.

Many of the things you are expected to do as Christian boys and girls are wearisome, uninteresting and monotonous. You are to keep on being pure in mind and heart; how uninteresting! You are to keep on loving your parents, friends and neighbors; how wearisome! You are to keep on saying your prayers; how monotonous! All these duties seem to be so unimportant that you sometimes wonder if they are really worth while, but you must believe that they are because they make you dependable. They are the very things that made Jesus dependable. He kept on being pure in heart and mind; he kept on loving; he kept on praying. That is why we can have faith in him. It may be rather a curious thing to say, nevertheless it is true, and that is that the purpose of our journey through life is not to get somewhere but to be something; and to set out on the Christian way simply means that we have made up our minds to become like Christ. He didn't get very far in the world but he became the Saviour of the world. So it is most important that you should "consider him . . . lest ye be wearied."

J. B. Wilson

98   *WHICH SIDE OF THE LINE?*

Have you read the story of Pizarro, the conqueror of Peru? You remember there came floating back to Spain wonderful tales of gold to be found in Peru; they even said that the rivers flowed over sands of gold. All you had to do was to pick it up out of the water. So Pizarro got together a company of men, fond of adventure and eager for gold, and together they braved the dangers of the Atlantic and crossed the Isthmus of Panama. But they had troublous times; on the sea there were storms, and on the land poisonous snakes and wild animals. The little company pushed their way south through the wilderness for a while, and then refused to go farther. "If you insist on going on," they said, "you will have to go alone; we are going back to Spain." Then Pizarro drew a line in the sand with his sword. They were on the north side of it, and he said, "Comrades, on that side of the line lie famine, perils, nakedness, and death; on this side, ease and pleasure. Choose as brave Spaniards. As for me, I go south," and he stepped over the line. Now what do you think they did? Every single man followed him. Why? Not for love of good, but for love of gold, and because they were afraid of being called cowards.

This story makes me think of how our Lord Jesus Christ laid down the line and said, "In this way you will have tribulations," and told what lay before him and before them. "If any man will come after me . . . let him . . . take up his cross, and follow me" (Matt. 16:24). Remember there was just one who went back, and that was Judas. Somehow we don't have very great admiration for Judas, do we? One was taken out, but the other eleven chose to follow Jesus.

Sometimes I wish it was not so easy to be a Christian in these days, and that you boys and girls had as hard a time as Pizarro's soldiers did. If it meant martyrdom to follow Jesus, as it did in the early Church; or persecution and the loss of home and friends, as it often does now in India, I am sure you would follow him, in spite of the cost. But every one of us has to make

the choice just the same today. Jesus draws the line and says,
"Will you choose the kingdom of God and his righteousness,
and live on that side, or will you choose for yourself?" And if
Pizarro's men followed him for the sake of gold, I am sure we
shall not hold back when Jesus asks us to follow him, not for
the sake of gold, but for the sake of his own righteousness and
the cause of righteousness in the world.

Edward MacArthur Noyes

99   *OUR UNSEEN HELPER*

Lo, I am with you alway. MATTHEW 28:20

From faraway Greece there comes to us the story of Theseus
and Ariadne. It is a tale of a hero who was helped in his greatest
battle by his unseen friend.

When Theseus, the hero of our story, was about ready to enter
the deep cavern to fight the terrible dragon, Ariadne ran up
to help him. She could not assist him by using a sword against
the dragon. She could not even go down into the cave with him
to cheer him in his contest against the terrible monster. She
had another plan to give him cheer in his dangerous task.

Ariadne tied a light, silk thread on the arm of Theseus. As
he went deeper and deeper into the dangerous cavern, Ariadne
unwound the silk thread. When Theseus finally entered into
combat with the monster, he felt the slight pressure of the
silk thread. Feeling the light touch of the thread, he thought
about Ariadne. He knew that she was cheering for him even
though he could neither see nor hear her. This gave him
courage. He felt stronger than ever. With renewed strength
he fiercely attacked the dragon and slew him. Bound to Ariadne

by a silk string, Theseus was victorious over his greatest enemy.

So it was in the life of Paul. One time when Paul was in the temple at Jerusalem, a mob of angry people attacked him. They dragged him violently out of the temple. People from all over town ran to see the excitement. Everything was in an uproar. Soon the chief captain of Jerusalem heard about the wild action of the mob. He rushed down with his soldiers and gave orders to bind Paul in chains and cast him into prison.

Things looked pretty dark for Paul in prison. You could hardly blame him if he felt downhearted, lonely, and discouraged.

But a wonderful thing happened to him during the night. In the dead silence of the night Paul knew that he was not alone: he felt the presence of his Unseen Friend. That is enough to refresh any drooping spirit. It filled the heart of Paul with cheer. The thrilling appearance of his Unseen friend is reported for us in the Bible, "And the night following the Lord stood by him, and said, Be of good cheer, Paul: for as thou hast testified of me in Jerusalem, so must thou bear witness also at Rome" (Acts 23:11). With his Unseen Friend constantly at his side, Paul was ready to go even to Rome.

Jesus promised, "Lo, I am with you alway." Paul found that Jesus is reliable: he always keeps his promise. The Unseen Friend stood by him even in prison!

There was another period in his life when Paul was cheered and strengthened by his Unseen Friend who stood by him. To get this story we must follow Paul to Rome.

Paul was taken to Rome as a prisoner. Instead of being cast into a dungeon Paul was given permission to live by himself, but a soldier had to stay at his side as a guard. During the many months that Paul had to wait for his case to come up for trial, he was not idle. He proclaimed the story of Jesus to everyone who would listen to him.

At last the day of trial came. All his friends had deserted him, and Paul had to stand up in court alone. When there is no one to back you up, you feel so terribly alone, and your stomach starts to cave in. You feel weak and faint. That is just the way Paul felt when he stood alone before the judge. Then he felt the gentle pressure of his Unseen Friend and everything was changed. No matter if everyone left him in the lurch, the Lord would not leave him: "The Lord stood with me and strengthened me" (2 Tim. 4:17). With the Lord Jesus at his side, Paul was strong enough for anything.

The Unseen Friend of Paul is also our Friend. We need such a Friend to stand by us and back us up if we would be good and true. Jesus knows our weakness. He must have been thinking about such a situation when he said, "Without me ye can do nothing" (John 15:5). Yes, we do feel helpless when we are all alone. But Jesus does not want us to be alone: he wants to be with us. If he stands back of us, we receive strength to stand for the right. Paul said, "I can do all things through Christ which strengtheneth me" (Phil. 4:13). And Jesus has promised to stand by us without fail: "Lo, I am with you alway."*

Karl H. A. Rest

100   *HOUSES*

Jesus talked a great deal about houses. He told stories about them. We do not wonder, for he was a carpenter and often built houses. He told a story of the good house that was built on the rock, and the poor house that was built on shifting sand. He said, "A house . . . divided against itself . . . cannot stand" (Mark 3:25), and Abraham Lincoln often used those words when he said that a nation that was half free and half slave would fall. Jesus said that heaven was a house of many mansions, many rooms, room enough for all. He once told a story about thieves breaking into a well-guarded house and binding the watchman and robbing the whole house. He told how necessary it is to keep watch, lest a thief come in the night. Once, when someone said he was going home with him, Jesus said that he had no home. He was homeless. He had no house of his own, but he was welcome in other people's houses. He was often a guest in Peter's house, and in the house at Bethany where his friends Mary and Martha and Lazarus lived.

Almost everything in the world has a house of its own. We may not call it a house but it is at least a place to live in. What do we call the house in which the President lives? Yes, the White House. What do we call the house the government lives in? Yes, the Capitol. What do we call a bird's house? Yes, a nest. And a lion's house? Yes, a den. And the house cattle live in? A stable. And sheep? A fold. And chickens? A coop. And a dog? A kennel. And fish? A pond or a river or a lake or the sea. And an automobile? A garage. And the house the minister lives in? A manse, if one is a Presbyterian; a parsonage, if one is a Methodist. And now here's a question you can't answer. What is the house a gossip lives in? Well, you call it a glass house, because people who live in glass houses shouldn't throw stones, that is, shouldn't tell tales. And what is the name of the house that had to do with

Houses

The maiden all forlorn,
That milked the cow with the crumpled horn,
That tossed the dog, that worried the cat,
That killed the rat, that ate the malt?

Yes! it is the house that Jack built. And what do you call the house where we worship? Yes! the church, the House of God. And what is the name of the house where you live? Why, yes, home! There are hundreds and thousands of houses and all of us possess two or three or four. Let us see.

There is the house I call my body. It is a good house. I have lived in it many years. Every one of us has a house that he calls his body. It may be a white, a black, a yellow or a brown house. It lasts a long while. The Bible says it lasts for threescore and ten years, that is, seventy years, perhaps eighty. It changes. Once this body which is my house could be held in a little child's arms and it weighed only seven or eight pounds. I don't remember exactly. Now it is too heavy for a man to lift. What a house it is! For windows it has eyes, for radios it has ears, for a loud-speaker it has a mouth, for an automobile it has legs. Who lives in this house? I do. Does anyone live with me? Yes, God lives with me, for the Bible says our bodies are his dwelling place.

Then there is the house I call my home. There is a difference between a house and a home. You can have a house and have no home, and you can have a home and have no house. One of the sad things Jesus said was about the foxes having holes and the birds of the air having nests but that he himself had nowhere to lay his head. We have a lovely hymn that says:

The foxes found rest,
And the birds their nest,

Jesus, the Children's Friend

In the shade of the forest tree;
But thy couch was the sod,
O thou Son of God,
In the deserts of Galilee:
O come to my heart, Lord Jesus,
There is room in my heart for thee.

What makes a home? I hardly know. It has been said that home is the place where we get three meals a day and our hearts a thousand. It is like this. A schoolteacher was helping the children build a house out of blocks and cardboard. When she was done, she said, "Now it is finished." "No," said one of the children, "it needs a mother." And that is a first-class definition of a home. And we know that the home Jesus lived in as a child had in it a beautiful mother, whose name was Mary, and your home, I am sure, has in it a beautiful mother.

There is the house called the world. What a big and beautiful house it is! It has a high roof, the sky. It has high and strong walls, the mountains. It has beautiful curtains, the clouds. It has the most lovely rugs in the world, the grass. It has magnificent light, the sun and moon and stars. It has many, many rooms—continents and islands and nations. It has wonderful showers, the rain. It has the biggest bathrooms in all the world, lakes and seas and oceans. It has music everywhere, the wind and the birds. Jesus loved this big beautiful house. He loved the sparrows and the lilies of the field, the moonlit nights and mountain silences.

Is there any other house? Yes, there is the house we call the church, God's House. When Jesus was a little boy the first place he visited when he went up to the big city was the church, the temple, which he called "my Father's house." And that is the way Jesus talked about heaven. He said, "In my Father's house are many mansions . . . I go to prepare a place for you" (John 14:2). How simple! How wonderful! Wherever God is, wherever our Lord Jesus Christ is, there is home, whether it is in this world or in the world to come. The world is "my Father's house" and heaven is "my Father's world" and they are both one world.

> This is my Father's world:
> He shines in all that's fair;
> In the rustling grass I hear him pass,
> He speaks to me everywhere.
>
> *Hugh Thomson Kerr*

101   *ENCOURAGEMENT FOR DONKEYS*

"Go, He said, to the village facing you, and immediately on entering it you will find an ass's foal tied up which no one has ever yet ridden: untie him and bring him here. And if anyone asks you, 'Why are you doing that?' say 'The Master needs it.' " MARK 11:2-3 (WEYMOUTH)

When you hear the lesson read on Palm Sunday, and hear how our Lord entered Jerusalem riding on a donkey, I expect you often think to yourself, "Well, what a funny animal to choose! Why a donkey, I wonder?" You would have expected a horse, wouldn't you? A horse is the sort of animal you expect a *king* to ride. Or if not a horse, then at least a camel—after all, you can manage to look quite dignified on a camel. But who can look dignified on a donkey? Even the greatest king that ever lived wouldn't quite look the part sitting on an animal like that. It makes you think of someone on vacation at the seaside, having a little jaunt along the sands—or of some poor peasant, who couldn't afford anything better.

But it wasn't an accident that our Lord rode in on a donkey. He chose to do so. He picked a donkey on purpose. For two reasons: in the first place, because it was a custom in those days, that when a king went to war, he rode on a horse—but if he came in peace, then he rode on a donkey. It was to show men what sort of a King he was: the Prince of Peace. Not at all the sort of king that men were expecting to see, when they heard the people shouting (as Luke 19:38 tells us they did shout), "Blessed be the King that cometh in the name of the Lord." They were looking for a king of the usual kind—one who had an army of well-armed soldiers behind him, and who could say, "Obey me, and do what I want you to do—or it will be the worse for you!" Whereas Jesus came gently and quietly—no bragging and sword rattling and threats—to recruit subjects and followers by quite a different method. The people he aimed to enlist were all to be people who *wanted to come,* and were eager to obey—not conscripts, who obeyed simply out of fear.

And in the second place, he wanted to act out that prophecy we find in the Book of Zechariah (9:9), from which all the Gospel writers quote: the passage where it says that the Messiah (God's special chosen messenger) will come to his people "meek, and sitting upon an ass." It was his way of telling them who he was: a last appeal to the whole city.

And, perhaps, woven in with these two thoughts was a third: the rabbis had a saying: "When Israel is unworthy, Messiah will come riding upon an ass." So it may be that, by entering Jerusalem in this way, our Lord was very gently reproving the people of his day, and telling them—in the most delicate manner possible—how very disappointed he was with them.

Christ the King, coming to enlist new followers—to proclaim his rule, and to invite all who would to become his subjects. That's what we see happening, as our Lord enters Jerusalem.

And who was the very first recruit, that day? *It was the donkey.* Not much of a follower; that, you may say with a laugh: ugly, with great big ears and rather moth-eaten fur, stupid and a slow runner—the exact opposite of a horse, which is a beautiful animal, well proportioned, with a sleek, shiny coat and fleet, powerful legs. But what are we told about this donkey? "The Lord hath need of him." He wasn't much to look at, he hadn't many gifts—but he was willing for Christ to use him!

God needs the clever people, and the brave people, and the gifted people, and the popular people whom everyone admires and is willing to follow. But he also needs "donkeys" like you and me—who are not much to look at, and who have little to give, but who are willing to do what we can and to do it gladly and faithfully. The people he wants most of all are the people who know that "the Lord has need of them," and who are swift to obey his call; the people who, like the old donkey on Palm Sunday, will go on steadily, whether they are greeted with cheers or with angry shouts—carrying him among men, that he may do his great work in the world.*

A. Whigham Price

102   *HE FACED DEATH TO SAVE OTHERS*

> Then Jesus told his disciples, "If any man would come after me, let him deny himself and take up his cross and follow me."
>
> MATTHEW 16:24 (RSV)

The sign of the Christian religion is the Cross. It reminds us of God who so loved us that he sent Jesus to be our Teacher, our Saviour and our Lord. He became our Saviour by dying on a cross so that our sins could be forgiven.

If you find it hard to understand the meaning of the Cross, you may know that no one has ever completely understood it. We cannot expect to be able with our little minds fully to comprehend God and his infinite love. The disciples themselves did not understand when Jesus announced to them that he "must go to Jerusalem, and suffer many things from the elders and chief priests and scribes, and be killed" (Matt. 16:21, RSV).

Jesus told those disciples: "If any man would come after me, let him deny himself and take up his cross and follow me." As the disciples accepted Jesus' invitation and tried to forget themselves and live for Christ and his cause, they came to understand better. Others who have tried have understood better, too.

This spirit of self-denial and sacrifice for the benefit of others is the mark of true heroism and the seal of a Christian. Not all who serve in this way do it in the name of Christ, but certainly they have a common spirit of concern for others.

To consider some of the deeds of the men who have been honored by membership in the Walter Reed Society may help us to illustrate this self-sacrificing spirit. All the members of this society have voluntarily endangered their lives to aid science to find cures for disease or in some way to help in the fight against the enemies of our health. One member allowed a cancerous cell to be transplanted into his own body in order that it might be studied. Another was injected with the virus of parrot fever in order that a way might be found to protect workers against this disease. Still another allowed his body to be terribly burned to test some new "wonder drugs."

Boy and Girl Scouts are familiar with the method used to revive a person who is unconscious and must be made to breathe artificially. The one you use today is not the one I was taught. It is a much better method, and more lives will be saved now.

Do you know how the new method was developed? It was made possible because a young medical student, Tom Koritz, was willing to become a human "guinea pig" while two famous doctors and their assistants experimented upon him. It is a story of courage, self-sacrifice and faith.

This was not the first time Tom Koritz had become a subject for a dangerous experiment. This time, however, was to be more serious than before. In order that Tom would be like an unconscious person needing artificial respiration, he was given an injection of curare. This is a poison. It was discovered years ago in South America where Indians used to put it on their arrows and blowgun darts. When such a poisoned arrow struck a person it would cause him to become paralyzed and helpless. He was unable to breathe. This meant, of course, that the victim would die.

Tom knew just what curare would do. He knew he was taking a big chance. He had faith in the doctors who would be experimenting with him, but he also knew that accidents could happen and that the experiment might be a failure. He might never regain consciousness. He was frightened, but he would not turn back.

The details of that experiment are many. A tube was run down Tom's throat so that oxygen could be pumped into his lungs. Instruments were attached to measure the amount of oxygen that could be pumped into his lungs by artificial respiration. The experiment was to find which of several methods was best in filling the lungs with oxygen and saving life.

You can imagine how sore Tom's body must have become as the assistants tried one method after another while he was paralyzed by the curare. You can also imagine how dizzy and sick Tom was when he finally regained consciousness. I say you can imagine, but really it is impossible for any of us to do that unless we have had the same thing happen to us. We are happy to know that Tom came through all right, and that today he is a practicing physician. He must be a very fine doctor and a very understanding one, for he has shown the spirit of self-sacrifice and service since those days when he was a student in college.

People sometimes ask Tom Koritz why he allowed himself to become a "guinea pig" and risk his life in these experiments. He is a modest doctor and he does not want to be called a hero, although everyone knows that he is. Tom says that when he was a small boy and the youngsters of the neighborhood were swimming in an old rock quarry, one of his pals was drowned. The local firemen tried to revive him by artificial respiration, but they failed. As Tom remembered that sad day he felt that his pal's life might have been saved if only a better method of lifesaving had been known. He wanted to do what he could to find that better method.

Tom feels that being a doctor is an honor as well as a responsibility and, to be worthy, a doctor must think always of others instead of himself. His spirit is like that of the Christian who denies himself as he follows Christ.

Julius Fischbach

103   *LOOK AT YOUR HANDS!*

I want each of you to look at your hands. No, I don't want you to inspect them for dirty fingernails or smudges. In fact,

Look at Your Hands!

I'm not even going to ask you to go wash them if you find a little bit of dirt here or there. I want you to think about the fact that your hands are your representatives in all of your work and play. The Bible says, "By their fruits ye shall know them," (Matt. 7:20). Isn't it true, however, that we can also say, "By our hands we are known"?

Your hands can be clenched into fists to hit the face of a boy or girl, or they can be opened up to clasp his or her hand in friendship. Your hands can be trained to hold a doctor's surgical instrument, or they can be used to drive a bayonet into someone's body. Your hands can be made to clutch the things you own like a miser does, or they can be opened as you give and share the things you possess. Your hands can fall hopelessly by your side as a symbol of your sadness and failure, or they can be raised with joy to picture your faith and hapiness. Surely it is true, "By our hands we are known."

And because this is true, we should pay more attention to our hands. Many boys and girls use their hands for little, unimportant things. But you can use your hands for good things. Especially, I would like to remind you of the hands of Jesus and how he used them.

The very first thing we remember about Jesus' hands is that they were Helpful Hands. Do you remember how, when Peter's mother-in-law had a fever, Jesus went to her house and put his hands upon her and made her well again? Surely you remember the time when the little girl was so sick that her father, whose name was Jairus, went to Jesus and asked him to heal her. Jesus went to the little girl's house, placed his hands upon her, and said, "Talitha cumi," which means, "Rise up, little one," and the child was healed. There was a man who could neither hear nor see. Jesus touched the blind eyes and the deaf ears. He said, "Ephphatha" or "Be opened," and the man could both hear and speak. Jesus used his hands as Helpful Hands all through his lifetime. When we read how he used his hands, we as Christians must go and do likewise.

How can our hands be Helpful Hands? Volunteering to help our mother with the dishes, or raking the leaves off the grass, or taking some little gift to a sick boy or girl will be ways by which we can use our hands as Jesus used his.

We remember also that Jesus' hands were Reverent Hands. Carefully and thoughtfully he picked up the Scriptures to read and to teach the Word of God. Often he folded his hands in prayer. Gently he picked a beautiful field flower or cupped his hands to hold a little bird. In these wonders of nature he saw the glory of God's skill and love made manifest.

Our hands will be Reverent Hands when we hold our Bibles as we go to church and when we turn the pages of God's Book. We show our reverence toward God when we clasp our hands in prayer and when we do any good deed in God's name and as Jesus would have done it. There were so many ways Jesus used his hands to express his love of God. Truly, by his hands he was known. At the time of his temptations and again in the Garden of Gethsemane, he folded his hands in prayer, the real power of his life. He used his hands to feed five thousand hungry people who had gone to him to hear his words of God. He used his hands to cleanse the Temple of the money-changers because he wanted his Father's House to be pure and holy.

But let us remember especially the last time those hands were ever used. That was the time they were stretched out on a cross with nails driven through them. I call those hands Sacrificial Hands. Jesus once said, "Greater love hath no man than this, that a man lay down his life for his friends" (John 15:13). That is exactly what he did. He loved people so much and his love was so great that bad men either had to become good and accept his love or else they felt that they must kill him. They determined to kill him, but through their evil intentions Jesus was able to express to mankind how much he really loved them. He loved men so much that he willingly died for them.

You children do not have to die for others, yet your hands can be Sacrifical Hands as you live for your friends. For we must make sacrifices, too. A sacrifice costs us something. It is not a sacrifice when we give away something we do not want. It is not a sacrifice to love those who love you. It is only when your giving and your loving mean real effort and cost you some self-denial that your hands are used sacrificially.

Yes, by our hands we are known. We can measure our love of Christ by the way we use our hands. So we must always take care to use them in the right ways. Are your hands Helpful Hands? Are they Reverent Hands? Are they Sacrificial Hands? Do your hands show your love for other boys and girls, your willingness to help them? Do your hands express your love for God? If so, you can be sure that you are using your hands in the right way.

Robert R. Brown

104   *THE VOICE THEY KNEW*

Jesus saith unto her, Mary. She turned herself, and saith unto him, Rabboni. JOHN 20:16

And it came to pass, as he sat at meat with them, he took bread, and blessed it, and brake, and gave to them. And their eyes were opened, and they knew him. LUKE 24:30-31

Jesus, the Children's Friend

Have you ever thought how queer it is that we human beings are all so different? I mean, there are millions of people in the world, and no two of them are alike: different faces, different voices, different minds, different ways of looking at things. If you are playing "Blind Man's Buff" and you catch hold of someone, it's almost impossible to guess who it is; but if the person you've caught gives a little giggle, the chances are that you'll recognize it. "That's Billy's giggle," you'll say. "You couldn't mistake it."

It's the same with voices. Sometimes when you go to see a play acted by people you know, someone comes on to the stage so well disguised that you can't tell who it is for the moment. But as soon as they speak, you know who it is right away. Or you may guess because of some little habit they've got—what is called a mannerism, like wrinkling their nose, or throwing back their hair with a toss of the head, or standing on one leg while talking. You can always tell a boy on the stage, even when he is dressed up in girl's clothes, because sooner or later he always tries to put his hands in his pockets when he's not speaking—at rehearsals, anyway—and then remembers, too late, that a girl's dress hasn't got any pockets, or at least not in the right place. No matter how different a person may *look,* his friends—the people who know him really well—will always recognize him. The real "you" always shines through, sooner or later.

All this helps us to understand what happened on the first Easter Day. Our Lord came to his friends in a *new* body, to prove to them that he was still alive, and that he would be their Friend for ever, even though they could not see him any more. He came in the new "body" which he would use in heaven—a new body for a different sort of life—just as a caterpillar has *one* body for crawling over cabbages and then, later on, a quite *new* body, a butterfly's body, for flying through the air from flower to flower, though it's really the *same* caterpillar inside the new body. What we've been saying about disguises explains two things that happened that first Easter morning: it explains how it was that Mary, who when she first met our Lord thought he was the gardener, *knew him at once* as soon as he spoke her name, just as you would know your father the moment he spoke *your* name, even if he were dressed up like Santa Claus with a long white beard. The voice could *only* be that of Jesus: he was alive after all!

And, secondly, it explains the end of the story of that walk to Emmaus, when the mysterious Stranger who had been their companion went in to supper with them. There was a certain way in which he broke the bread which made it clear to them that it could only be Jesus, and no one else. These little things made them quite sure.

We can't see Jesus, either, but we can always hear him speak, in our hearts. We call it "conscience"—but the voice is his; it can't possibly be anyone else's. He calls us by name, as he called Mary; and, when you are a little older, he will call you, too, to share in his gifts at his Holy Table—to receive what he has blessed, to make you strong.

A. Whigham Price

15. *SPIRIT OF THANKFULNESS*

❦

We hear a great deal about the Pilgrim Fathers who came over to this country from England in the *Mayflower* and settled at Plymouth, Massachusetts. We hear less about the Pilgrim Mothers who suffered all the hardships of cold and hunger, Indians and disease, with them. If you ever go to Plymouth to see Plymouth Rock, where it is said our Pilgrim Fathers first stepped ashore at Plymouth, I hope you will walk a little way down the beach and look at the lovely statue of the Pilgrim Mother. There she stands, looking out toward the sea, in her homespun dress and her heavy shoes. This statue seems to me more beautiful than any statue of the Pilgrim Fathers I have ever seen.

But we hear still less of the Pilgrim Children than we do of their fathers and mothers. What were they like? I suppose they were like all other boys and girls at heart, but they lived in a different time. They lived in a country in which there were deer and wolves and bears and wild turkeys, a country of forests and Indians. There were no roads, no automobiles, no telephones, no railroads. They lived in log cabins and went to church in log churches. There were no glass windows in those early churches. They used waxed paper for windowpanes. There were no stoves. Some people carried foot stoves, with charcoal on the inside, to keep their feet warm. The women and girls and little children sat on one side of the church, the men and boys on the other. There was a tithingman at the church service. He had a long pole with a fox's tail at one end and a sharp prick at the other. If he saw a woman asleep during the service, he tickled her nose with the fox's tail. If he saw a man asleep, he pricked him with the other end. They used to nail bearskins and wolfskins along the front of the pews in some of the churches, like a pocket, so that the little children could put their feet in them and keep warm. The sermons were very long, generally over an hour. After morning service, people ate lunch at the church. Then came Sunday school, and after that another preaching service.

Since there were no roads, people had to walk to church or ride on horseback. The husbands carried guns to protect their wives and children from the Indians. When there were too many in a family to ride horseback they would "ride and tie." This meant that those on horseback would ride ahead, and the others walk along behind. When those riding got to a suitable place they would get off and tie the horse and walk on ahead. When those on foot came where the horse was they would ride him awhile and then tie him for the others to catch up.

It was hard work getting to church, and on cold winter days uncomfortable sitting in church. But these Pilgrim Fathers came to this country to worship God in their own way, un-molested by bishops or kings or magistrates, and I suppose it seemed like heaven to them to be at liberty to have the kind of church they liked. We sometimes forget all they suffered. I don't think it seemed much of a hardship to worship in a cold church, but we would think we were treated badly if we had to put up with it. We ought to be very thankful that we can come to a beautiful church, heated and lighted, with none to make us afraid. When we feel like complaining about some little discomfort, perhaps it will help us to remember what the Pilgrim Children went through.

Howard J. Chidley

106   *I PREFER THE NECK*

It was the Sunday before Thanksgiving. The Harris family, a nice big one, was having chicken for dinner.

"Mother," asked Dad as usual when there were children, "what piece will you have?"

"I'll wait for the last, Henry," replied Mother as she always did, "and I prefer the neck."

Dad carved off the neck, added a piece of white meat to it and passed the plate down to her.

Ben, the oldest of the Harris children, looked at his mother's face in perplexity. Did Mother really like the neck so well? The few times Ben had even tried it he had found that part of the chicken rather poor picking. It seemed to be all joints.

Although he was devouring his drumstick busily, Ben took time to watch his mother's patient efforts to get every bit of meat from the piece she had requested. Why did she always ask for the neck? he kept wondering.

He looked around the table at his five brothers and sisters and thought he knew the answer: she wanted all of them to have the best pieces.

After dinner, when the boys and girls were washing and wiping the dishes, Ben held a conference.

"Listen, everybody! You remember how every time Dad carves a chicken and asks Mother what part she'll have, she always says, 'I prefer the neck, Henry.'"

Everybody nodded. They remembered all right. The rest of them spoke right out for drumsticks, second joints, wishbones, and even for livers, but Mother always got the neck.

"Well, who wants to join the Thanksgiving Club for curing her of always taking the neck?" continued Ben.

"I," said Margie.

"Sure," said Dick.

"Let me in on it," nodded Bill.

Even little Lucy and Henry Junior clamored to help.

Then Ben confided the secret which he had just been making up. It set all their eyes to dancing with delight.

"Don't you tell," he cautioned the youngest pair.

"We won't," they promised, gleefully.

Wednesday afternoon the Harris children were bent on strange errands which took them to their nearby relatives and other close friends. These visits caused some surprise and many hearty chuckles, to say the least. But, after all, you never could tell what fun those Harris kids would concoct. There were so many of them that what one didn't think of, another did.

The Thanksgiving Day service at the church was a lovely one. At the insistence of the entire family, Mother had left the dinner arrangements in Margie's hands. It was the first time that had ever happened, and Mother truly enjoyed sitting in the family pew with her children.

The pastor spoke of some of the gifts for which one should be grateful and the choir sang a beautiful anthem of Thanksgiving. Mother could scarely keep back the tears as she glanced at her happy family and thought of their solicitude for her. If she worried about the dinner at home, she gave no indication of concern.

There was no cause for worry about that dinner. Margie did her work splendidly, and Ben and the others ably supported her when they got home from church.

Mother felt very much the guest of honor as her daughter announced that dinner was ready. At sight of the dancing eyes of her little brood, she thought it was surely because for the first time in their lives they had been allowed to prepare the holiday dinner. It was grand of them, she thought proudly.

Though the potatoes were slightly burned, and the bread cut in rather thick and uneven slices, the table presented a fine appearance when the children ushered their father and mother to their places.

Father gave a hearty prayer of Thanksgiving while all sat with bowed heads.

After the soup was consumed with relish, Bill, with Margie's help, bore in the big platter with the chicken.

Dad flourished his carving knife and fork and looked down the table toward Mother. "Emily, what portion?" he asked.

Came the familiar words, "I'll wait till the last, Henry, and I prefer the neck."

As Father obediently laid her plate aside, the children could hardly keep from laughing.

"Margie, what will you have?"

"The neck, please, Dad."

Mr. Harris carved off the neck and passed it to his daughter.

"Lucy?" he continued.

"May I have a neck, please, Daddy?"

Mysteriously another neck appeared and was deposited on her plate.

"Bill, what'll you have?"

"Neck, please."

Father speared another neck and laid it on Bill's plate beside the mashed potatoes.

From her end of the table Mother was regarding the proceedings with eyes that opened wider and wider. As the game went on with Ben, Dick, Henry Junior, and Henry Senior all receiving fine, well-browned chicken necks, the dear lady's face became very pink. Her eyes grew a bit misty for a minute, then she broke out into gales of laughter.

When she finally found voice to speak, she exclaimed, gaily, "I hadn't the least idea that that chicken had seven necks or I'd have sold him to a museum."

"It is a remarkable chicken," agreed Dad, making a great pretense of searching all over the platter for still another neck. "But unfortunately there doesn't seem to be any left for you, Emily. What would your second choice be?"

"I'll take the wishbone, please," replied the mother steadily, "and then, if you'll join me, Henry, we'll wish that when our children are grown up they'll have as much to be thankful for as we have."

After that Thanksgiving Day, Mrs. Harris did not for a long time request her usual portion of chicken, although there may have been some truth in what Dick said, when they were washing the dishes of that memorable dinner: "You know, she loves us so much, always wanting us to have the best, that I guess maybe she really did prefer the neck."

Paul Franklin Swarthout

107 *THE PIE THAT TOOK A THOUSAND MEN TO MAKE*

Uncle John invited the whole family to eat Thanksgiving Day dinner at his home: Father, Mother, Mary and Claude. The family loved Uncle John and always looked forward eagerly to a visit at his home in the country. This year he wrote, "Tell Claude that we are going to have a mince pie that took a thousand men to make."

Claude opened his eyes wide. At first he said, "I don't believe that a pie that took a thousand men to make could get into the house. It would be higher than the ceiling. It would need a ladder to climb to the top and cut it."

His father said: "Uncle never makes a promise that he fails to keep. It must be so." Claude could hardly wait for Thanksgiving Day to come, he was so anxious to see and taste that wonderful pie. He thought, "Why, the slices will be so big even a boy will have all the pie he wants for once. But my! I will have to eat sparingly of the first part of the dinner to enjoy that huge piece of pie."

At last Thanksgiving morning arrived. Silverboots, the dog, was left with a neighbor; Mary took her doll, Arabella; Claude drove from the garage the car he had helped his father to polish; Mother got the suitcases ready, and all set off for Uncle John's to see and enjoy the big mince pie. When they arrived, and the rest had gone in the house, Claude peeped into the barn and shed and other places outside to see if he could find the pie; then he peeped in the kitchen, the dining room and everywhere he thought the pie might be stored; but he saw no sign of it.

When the dinner hour came, all sat around the table enjoying the turkey and all the good things that went with it. Claude said, "I must be careful not to eat too much now or I won't have room for the pie." He was happy when the first courses were finished and the moment arrived when the pie was to be served.

Claude raised his eyes in expectation as Uncle John said, "Now for the pie." How his eyes fell when his aunt brought in an ordinary mince pie—only just a little larger than usual.

"Uncle John, that pie didn't take a thousand men to make!" cried Claude.

"Hold on," replied Uncle smiling, "not so fast. Yes, that pie did take a thousand men to make."

"How could it?" said Claude.

"Well," said Uncle, "what is this pie made of?"

Claude replied, "Flour, sugar and—"

"Yes," said Mary, "and spice, suet, meat, apples, molasses— and, oh, a great many other things too."

"Begin with the flour," said Uncle. "Where did the flour come from?"

"The farmer, the miller, the baker, the grocer."

"Yes," said Uncle, "and the men to make the plows and mills and ovens and stores. And so on with the sugar, spice, and all the rest. Think of the implements, tools, machinery and the men it took to make them; think of the railroad trains, steamships, autos, trucks, wagons to transport these articles. Now add all together and you will find a thousand men had each his part in making this Thanksgiving pie—besides Aunt Sue. She couldn't have made it but for all the rest."

Claude's face beamed as he said: "I never once thought of that before! We ought to think of all this when we eat a piece of pie."

"But," Uncle John continued, "it took a thousand men to make this pie—and one woman; but it took more; whom else did it take?"

"Oh, I know," exclaimed Claude, "it took God, too."

"You are right again, Claude," answered Uncle, "and back and behind all is God. Let us remember:

> Back of the loaf is the snowy flour,
>   And back of the flour, the mill;
> And back of the mill is the wheat and the shower,
>   And the sun, and the Father's will."

William James Sly

108 *A PREACHER WITH FOUR EYES*

When I sat at my desk one evening last week, I was greeted by a large friendly-looking potato. As fine a specimen as I had seen for a long time, I thought. On his left side was an attached label, on which was written, in a childish hand: "Please say something about me next Sunday morning, in your talk to the girls and boys!"

I asked my new companion if he would kindly tell me what to say. I felt sure that he was able to do that. So it came about that he talked—in his own way, of course—and I listened—in my way. As he spoke slowly and clearly, I was able to write down every word of his interesting talk. This is what he said, or, perhaps I should say, a part of what he said.

"I am known by several names. Some people call me Murphy: others call me Spud. My proper name, however, is Potato. There are about a thousand varieties belonging to our great family. I am told that the Deadly Nightshade and the Tobacco plant claim to belong to our tribe. I think you will agree with me when I say that they are not so useful as we are. If you cut me open (I shan't mind that), and look at me through a microscope, you will see that I am wonderfully made. No one but God could have made me so wonderful, and, if I may say so, so beautiful. My life story is a most interesting one. I was first brought to this country, I understand, nearly four hundred years ago. (I am speaking of my forefathers, of course.) I was well known in South America long before I was introduced to your people here. I have many enemies and they keep on trying to destroy me. But there are more of us in the world today than ever before. And, according to what I hear, there'll be many, many more of us next year

"I am told by those who know, that I have been the means of saving millions of lives. Perhaps you won't believe it, but it is true that when I first arrived in your land I was given what is called the cold shoulder. Few people were willing to give me house room. Of course the others didn't know who or what I was. Later, however, men and women, and children, too, got to like me, and to value me. Then I began to make history, whatever that means. (I'm telling you what I have heard.)

"I have fed multitudes down the years. In times of famine, I understand, I have played a noble part. Some say that I am not as nourishing as wheat. They had better not repeat that in the hearing of the Food Minister. He would surely have them up for causing despondency, or alarm, or both.

"I hope you won't think that I am boasting foolishly when I tell you that, the other day, I was given a place of honor at a Ministry of Health exhibition, and that the people who know what's what, commended me to all the world. They said that I was excellent food, and they spoke of my calories and my vitamins. What they meant by those strange words I don't know, but I believe they stand for necessary and valuable things. That's more than can be said of beer and ale, and that sort of thing. These drinks have little or no value, and so they were not so much as mentioned among the things we must have if we are to carry on. As I came through the city, this morning, I saw placards declaring that 'Beer Is Best.' If that claim is true, why wasn't it given a place of honor in that Food Exhibition? That's what I'd like to know.

"I have heard it said that one day motorcars will be run on fuel obtained from potatoes. I should welcome that idea, so long as the people's food was not interfered with. I hope they'll never degrade me by turning me into alcohol for making people drunk. If that should come to pass, I hope that all the members of our distinguished order will go on strike, and refuse to grow at all. That would show them."

My friend stopped there. Then he looked at me with his four eyes, as if to say: "I think I've said enough." I told him that we were pleased that he always came to our harvest thanksgiving services and that we gave thanks to God for him, because he was the friend of everybody, and especially of the poor. Here he smiled, and whispered: "Chips!"

I invited him to accompany me to church on Sunday morning, and I promised that our children would be pleased to see him, and that they would listen with interest to his story of himself, and to his words of advice and warning. I added that I would like to be sure that all of us were as useful in our way as he was in his way; and that I was glad that I didn't live here over four hundred years ago. At that I thought I discerned a twinkle in his smallest eye, and a smile on his rugged old face.

J. R. Edwards

16. THE MEANINGS OF CHRISTMAS

❦

109   *I'LL SHOW YOU*

"He who has seen me has seen the Father." JOHN 14:9 (RSV)

One Saturday afternoon a little boy named Jimmy was watching his father work on the engine of the family automobile. His father was leaning over the front fender and was pounding with his hammer and twisting with his wrench. Finally he straightened up, and he turned to his son. "Jimmy," he said, "I need a new distributor head. Run over to the garage and get one for me, will you?"

Jimmy was glad to be able to help his father, but on the way to the garage he forgot the words "distributor head." "Oh, well," he said to himself, "it doesn't really matter. I know what it looks like."

So when Jimmy got to the garage, he told the man what he wanted. It was something about as big as this, which went on the engine either on the right side or on the left side. He couldn't remember which side. "I think I know what you mean," the garageman said, and he gave Jimmy a carburetor.

"No," said Jimmy, "that isn't it." Jimmy began his description all over again. "It's not very big," he said, "and maybe, after all, it doesn't go on the side of the engine. Maybe it fits on top."

"I have it now!" said the garageman, and he gave Jimmy a spark plug.

Jimmy shook his head. "That isn't what I need."

The garageman made other suggestions, but none were right. Finally, Jimmy gave up. "You wait here a minute," he said. "I'll go back and get the old one. Then I'll show you what I mean." So Jimmy got the worn-out part and took it back to the garage.

"Why didn't you say that was what you wanted?" the man asked. "That's a distributor head. Here you are! Take it back to your father."

God sent Jesus to the earth so that men might know what God was like. For hundreds of years God had tried to tell people what he was like. Through Moses he gave people the Ten Commandments, and in them he tried to explain what kind of God he was. Then through Amos he told people that he was a God of justice who hated evil and sin. Still later through a man named Hosea he told the world that he was a God of love. But people did not seem to understand. They were not sure what God was like. So at last God said, "I shall stop trying to explain myself to men. I'll *show* them." Then he sent Jesus to the earth. Jesus was God's own Son. People who saw Jesus would know that God was like him. Jesus said, "He who has seen me has seen the Father." He meant by that that God and Jesus are just alike.

We know that God is kind because Jesus was kind. We know that God is good because Jesus was good. We know that God can conquer all of the evil in the world because, even when evil men killed Jesus, they could not put an end to him. Since Jesus came to the earth, we know what God is like because Jesus showed us.

Roy M. Pearson

110   *GOD'S MIRROR*

The dayspring from on high hath visited us. LUKE 1:78

When you are reading you like best the books that have pictures in them. Let me tell you an illustration to set alongside this text. It is a picture in a palace in Rome. The picture is called *Aurora,* the Dawn. In it you see the dark sky of early morning. Away in the west is nothing but darkness and a few stars breaking through. In the east there is a bank of dark clouds, but something is happening there. On the horizon is a golden chariot coming up through the clouds and driving away the darkness. It is the chariot of the lady Aurora, the goddess of the dawn. That is a picture that men thought about, hundreds of years before Jesus came into the world at Bethlehem, but I believe that the man who first outlined it perhaps saw far away a kind of dim vision of Jesus. A God who cared so much for us that he would send the dawn every morning to chase away the darkness must be a very kind God, just the loving God who would send Jesus to drive away darkness from the world. In Jesus the dayspring from on high hath visited us.

There is another startling thing about the picture. It is in a curious place—not on the walls of the palace, but on the ceiling! It is very hard to get a good view of it. You stand craning your neck and looking up, as if you were watching an airplane in the sky. It is difficult to get a proper view of it and to see how beautiful it is. You might go away disappointed, but then you notice something. In the center of the room is a table. And the top of the table is made not of wood but of looking-glass. It is a big mirror right underneath the middle of the roof. And, when you look into it, lo and behold! you see the picture reflected, every line in it clear and plain.

Does that not make us think of Jesus? For hundreds and hundreds of years God seemed so far off. Men looked up to the sky and watched and wondered. But they could never be sure how much of God they had really seen, and whether they had seen him clearly. When they came away they were not very sure whether they really knew what he was like. But one day, on the first Christmas morning, there came into the world a Child who was to be the perfect mirror, in whom they were at last to see the whole beautiful picture. And the mirror was Jesus. "Now," they said, "we have seen God; now we know what he is like; now we know how good and wonderful he is." And they had a word for it. They said, "Immanuel." They made it out of three words—*Im, anu, El*—with, us, God. Immanuel: God with us.*

Edgar Primrose Dickie

111   *THE YEAR ONE*

Once upon a time there was a Year One. Strangely enough, it was not the beginning of the years. The world was already very old; nobody knows how old. People had been living on the earth, time out of mind, in mighty nations, fighting great battles and building great cities. But somehow, everything seemed to begin over again that year, because that was when the King came. And we have taken it ever since as the most important of all dates. When we say that this present year is nineteen-hundred-and-something, we mean that the Year One was just so many years ago.

The Year One

It is always to be remembered about that year that one of its days was Christmas Day.

You may not think that strange. Christmas comes so regularly every year, like apples in autumn and snow in winter, that it seems to belong to the order of nature, and one may easily imagine that it has been celebrated always, and that it is as old as boys and girls. But the truth is that there was never any Christmas till the Year One.

Year after year, and year after year, the evergreen trees grew in the woods and nobody came to get them. Nobody thought of lighting them up with candles or of loading them down with candies. The holly showed its berries of red and the mistletoe its berries of white, and nobody paid any attention to them, except perhaps the Druids, whoever they were, and they had never heard of Christmas. The twenty-fifth day of December came and went, like the twenty-second and the twenty-ninth; and boys and girls were born and grew up into men and women with never a Christmas carol nor a Christmas tree nor a Christmas gift, and without having so much as heard of the singing angels or of the Holy Child; because that was before the King came.

Now, in the Year One, there lived in a quiet little place, in a small village hidden among hills, a young girl named Mary. One day, Mary was sitting alone in her room. She may have been reading; for we know that she loved to read. A poem which she wrote, called the Magnificat, is full of the memories of books. Or, she may have been sewing; for she was presently to be married, and would be getting ready for the wedding. She was to marry a neighbor, the village carpenter, named Joseph. It was a spring morning, and the flowers were in blossom, and the birds were singing, and the sun was shining. Thus she sat, with her heart full of beautiful thoughts, when of a sudden such a gleam of splendor shone about her that it seemed as if the sun had been under a thick cloud and had just come out and begun to blaze in good earnest. Mary turned to see where this new brightness came from; and there beside the door, dressed all in white, stood a resplendent angel.

The angel said, "Hail, thou that art highly favored, the Lord is with thee: blessed art thou among women." And Mary was afraid, and began to tremble; so that the angel said, "Fear not, Mary: for thou hast found favor with God" (Luke 1:28, 30). Then, while she held her breath and listened, he told his wonderful errand. God had seen the sin and sorrow that were upon the earth, he had heard little children, and even grown men and women, fathers and mothers, crying. He knew how people were trying to be good and making a sad failure of it because they were ignorant or weak. And now God was about to do what he had long promised: he was to come and live among us. God had, indeed, lived among men always, as he does today. Always and everywhere we are in the presence of God. But now he was to make himself known in a new way. The King of Glory was to take our human nature upon him, and become a man like us. He was to come, not in his royal robes of splendor, not in the garments of the sunset, not with his holy angels with him, but as a little child, to be born as we are, to grow as we grow, and thus by living our life to teach us how to live. And when the King came in his humility, Mary was to be his mother.

And Mary said, "Behold the handmaid of the Lord; be it unto me according to thy word" (Luke 1:38). Then the angel departed from her. That was the first day of the Year One.*

George Hodges

112   THE MEETING OF THE TREES

Many years ago when the first flurries of snow were falling, the trees of all the forests decided to do something to make Christmas a still happier day. So they held a great meeting in a large forest of the North to see what gift they could give to mankind on Christmas Day. Every kind of tree was present, and they all agreed that a big oak tree was to preside at the meeting.

At once the oak called the meeting to order. This is what he said: "My dear fellow trees, I am happy to see so many of you here. We have something very important to decide today. Soon it will be Christmas. That is a day of giving gifts, so we also want to give something. Besides God, we trees are man's oldest friends and with our branches we wave gladness to them. We are older than man and we live longer. I think we receive our greatest joy in giving and certainly Christmas is a time of giving. We enrich the soil with our falling leaves, we give shade, and in our shade we cause the clear water to come to the surface to quench man's thirst. We give lumber to mankind for their homes to shield them from the cold of winter and the heat of summer. We supply the wood to heat their homes; and some of us grow the fruit for man to eat."

To everything the oak said, the other trees nodded their heads in agreement.

"It will not be easy," continued the oak, "to find a gift appropriate for Christmas."

With this they also agreed, and then there followed a long discussion as to what they could do that would add to the happiness of all people at Christmas. The stately elm listened with a great deal of interest. Finally he asked the oak for permission to make a suggestion.

"It seems to me," said the elm, "that we could make the various families happiest if one of us would go directly into their homes to spend the Christmas holidays with them."

"Yes," added the maple tree, "we could also be in their churches and on the streets of their villages and cities spreading Christmas cheer."

"These suggestions are very good," said the tall pine tree, "but who of us will volunteer to do this?"

Then the oak tree said, "I think we should not ask for a volunteer, we ought to select a tree best suited to represent the spirit of Christmas."

"And what tree is that?" asked the oak.

This question was followed by a long silence as the chilly northern wind swayed the branches of all the trees as if to stir them into action. The trees looked at one another wondering which one would receive the honor of spending the Christmas holidays in the homes of the many families.

Then the hickory tree asked for permission to speak. "As I look at myself and all of us here," he said, "I notice that the leaves have fallen from all of our branches, but there is one tree among us that is always green both winter and summer."

No sooner had the hickory tree said this, than all of the trees looked at the evergreen. There the evergreen stood in all her beauty, the needles as green as in summer, with a sparkle of pure white snow upon her branches. The other trees recognized at once that the evergreen should become the Christmas tree to cheer the hearts of young and old.

The linden tree approvingly nodded his head, saying, "The evergreen is the only one among us that can bring living green foliage to our friend man, when the winter winds blow and snow covers the ground."

"But my choice of the evergreen has reasons even deeper than that," continued the hickory.

"What are those reasons?" asked the oak, the chairman of the meeting.

"The evergreen represents what Christmas should mean to our friends, the girls and boys, the men and women," replied the hickory. "She will fill the homes with fragrance in the cold, bleak winter. Christmas means that when the world was dark, dreary and cruel, God gave his Son Jesus to make it a happier and more beautiful place. Jesus has made the world happier and better with the fragrance of his beautiful life.

"Not only that," continued the hickory, "the fact that the evergreen is always green means that Jesus came to bring us everlasting life. The needles on the evergreen do not die in winter, and people who take Jesus as their Saviour live forever with him in heaven. That is what Christmas means. 'God so loved the world, that he gave his only begotten Son, that whosoever believeth in him should not perish, but have everlasting life' (John 3:12).

"Also, the evergreen has the shape of a spire, pointing upward to God," added the hickory. "It will remind all men that Jesus came on Christmas Day to point all men to God."

The evergreen was the unanimous choice of all the trees. She thanked them all for the honor which they had bestowed upon her. And ever since then the evergreen has been the symbol of Christmas. The meeting of the trees was adjourned. They had added much to the Christmas cheer.

Jacob J. Sessler

113   *HIS DAY—NOT OURS*

If I were to ask you whose birthday we celebrate on Christmas, you would say, "It is Christ's birthday that we celebrate." And that would be the right answer, for Christmas is Christ's day. It is his birthday. That is the most important thing to remember about Christmas. It is his day, and not ours.

That is something which is easy to say, but it is not as easy to live by. A minister was visiting in the home of some friends on Christmas Day. Naturally, he expected to find a scene of merriment and jollity. But he was disappointed. The little boy in the home had not received the present he had set his heart on. He had wanted a bicycle and, although he had been given many splendid and wonderful gifts, he was sulking and wrathful. His behavior greatly distressed his parents and they, too, were saddened. They had thought carefully about the matter and had felt that the boy was not yet old enough for a bike.

This little boy who found no joy in Christmas had forgotten one thing which is necessary to have a happy Christmas. He had forgotten that Christmas is Christ's day, not his day.

Let us remember Christ on his day. We must remember how he came as a tiny baby, how he grew up in a little village where he worked in his father's shop, how he went out among men as a teacher and a friend, a healer and a helper, and at last how he gave himself on the Cross to save us and then rose from the grave in eternal triumph. No wonder the heavens opened and the angels sang at the hour of his birth! Let us think of him and not of ourselves, and praise him with happy songs and cheerful spirits. For Christmas is his day—not ours.

Lowell M. Atkinson

114   *I WOULD BE TRUE*

Away up in the hills of China a young missionary sat thinking of Christmas and of his mother. He wanted to send a gift to her, and there was nothing to buy. What would she think if nothing came from across the sea to remind her that her boy, Howard, was thinking of her and loving her just as much as ever! As he looked away across the valley to the great mountains in the distance, he thought how good that mother had been to him; of his happy days in school and at home, and then of the opportunity his mother had given him to study at one of the great American universities—Princeton.

"Mother has been such a good mother to me," he said. "I wish I could do something to make her happy. I wish I could buy something lovely to send to her." Then, like a flash, there came the second thought: "Mother doesn't care for things that you can buy with money. She never did. She cares for what I am; not for what I can buy. She used to be proud of the little verses that I wrote when in college. I know she saved them, every one. I'll just write a little poem all for her, telling her some things that she wants to know."

Out came his pencil, and he began to scribble on a bit of paper. He wrote a few lines, and then erased them. That wasn't good enough for his mother. He tried again; slept on the thought; added a little now and then. Finally he copied what he had written and sent it in a letter to America. It was on its way for more than six weeks, and Christmas grew nearer and nearer.

Now, Christmastime is a lonesome time when the ones you love are far away, and Mrs. Walter, his mother, was looking anxiously for a letter from China. She was sure that it would not be late, for Howard never forgot. Her face shone when it finally came, and she sat down in an easy chair to enjoy it.

Strange to say, it did not begin, "Dear Mother," as usual. Instead his mother read:

A Christmas Gift to Mother

I would be true, for there are those who trust me;
I would be pure, for there are those who care;
I would be strong, for there is much to suffer;
I would be brave, for there is much to dare.

I would be friend of all—the foe, the friendless;
I would be giving, and forget the gift;
I would be humble, for I know my weakness;
I would look up, and laugh, and love, and lift.

"What could be a nicer Christmas gift?" thought the mother of that young missionary away off in China, as she read it over and over. "It is too beautiful to keep all to myself. I will share it with the world."

Soon she sent the poem to Harper's, and they were eager to print it in their magazine. Publishers saw it, and wanted to copy it. Musicians read it, and knew that a great hymn had been found. Ministers used it in their talks to young people, and were glad that it had come from a young man to the youth of America. Finally it was put into the hymnbooks, and young people all over the world, today, are singing the words that Howard Arnold Walter sent as a Christmas gift to his mother:

I would look up, and laugh, and love, and lift.

Margaret W. Eggleston

SOURCES

The sources for reprinted materials are identified by story-sermon numbers.

1 *Solid Sunshine*, London: Epworth Press, 1939, pp. 15 ff.
2 *The Junior Church in Action*, New York: Harper & Brothers, 1921, pp. 78 ff.
6 *Thirty Stories I Like to Tell*, New York: Harper & Brothers, 1949, pp. 19 ff.
7 *The Children's Year*, Westwood, New Jersey: Fleming H. Revell, 1916, pp. 52 ff.
9 *Children's Sermons*, Philadelphia: Westminster Press, 1954, pp. 28 ff.
15 *Ibid.*, pp. 55 ff.
16 *Story Sermons and Plans for the Junior Church*, New York: Abingdon Press, 1949, pp. 52 f.
18 *A Year with the Children*, New York: Abingdon Press, 1937, pp. 35 ff.
20 *The Knight and the Dragon*, London: Robert Scott, 1914, pp. 53 ff.
22 *The Armour of Light*, London: Independent Press, 1951, pp. 56 ff.
24 *Story Sermons from Literature and Art*, New York: Harper & Brothers, 1939, pp. 17 f.
25 *Doing the Impossible*, London: Independent Press, 1951, pp. 74 f.
26 *The Armour of Light*, op. cit., pp. 7 ff.
30 *More Sermon Trails for Boys and Girls*, New York: Harper & Brothers, 1946, pp. 43 ff.
31 *A Million Miles to Nowhere*, London: Independent Press, 1951, pp. 40 ff.
32 *Wits End Corner*, London: Epworth Press, 1937, pp. 53 f.
33 *Children of God*, Philadelphia: Muhlenberg Press, 1934, pp. 113 f.
35 *More Sermon Trails for Boys and Girls*, op. cit., pp. 72 ff.
36 *One Year's Talks to Children*, Westwood, New Jersey: Fleming H. Revell Co., n. d., pp. 46 ff.
37 *New Story Talks to Boys and Girls*, New York: Harper & Brothers, 1929, pp. 74 f.
38 *The Church and the Children*, New York: Morehouse-Gorham Co., Inc., 1941, pp. 187 f.
39 *Ladders to the Sun*, New York: Abingdon Press, 1939, pp. 15 ff.
40 *Castles in the Air*, London: Independent Press, 1948, pp. 37 f.
42 *The Children's Story Garden*, ed. by Anna Pettit Broomell, Philadelphia: J. B. Lippincott Co., 1935, pp. 186 f.
45 *A Million Miles to Nowhere*, op. cit., pp. 67 f.
46 *105 Modern Parables for Young Folks*, Boston: W. A. Wilde Co., 1940, p. 95.
47 *Story Sermons from Literature and Art*, op. cit., pp. 44 f.

Sources

49 *The Teakwood Pulpit and Other Stories for Junior Worship*, New York: Abingdon Press, 1950, pp. 43 ff.

50 *100 Tales Worth Telling*, London: James Clarke & Co., Inc., 1947, pp. 157 f.

51 *Junior Sermon Stories*, Westwood, New Jersey: Fleming H. Revell Co., 1942, pp. 57 ff.

53 *The King Who Polished His Crown*, London: Independent Press, 1949, pp. 69 ff.

54 *Traffic Lights*, London: Epworth Press, 1938, pp. 40 ff.

55 *Children's Gospel Story-Sermons*, Westwood, New Jersey: Fleming H. Revell Co., 1921, pp. 130 ff.

57 *All-the-Year Stories*, ed. by Elsie H. Spriggs, Westwood, New Jersey: Fleming H. Revell Co., 1928, pp. 120 ff.

58 *Stewardship Stories*, New York: Harper & Brothers, 1941, I, 85 ff.

61 *Successful Fund Raising Sermons*, ed. by Julius King, New York: Funk & Wagnalls Co., 1953, pp. 59 f.

62 *Listen, My Children*, Westwood, New Jersey: Fleming H. Revell Co., 1944, pp. 35 ff.

63 *Stewardship Stories*, op. cit., II, 18 ff.

64 *The Second Book of Story Talks*, New York: Round Table Press, 1936, pp. 139 f.

65 *Listen, Children!*, London: Epworth Press, 1948, pp. 100 ff.

66 *Sixty Story Sermons for Boys and Girls*, New York: Abingdon Press, 1938, pp. 37 ff.

68 *Stewardship Stories*, op. cit., II, 33 f.

69 *A Year of Children's Sermons*, New York: Abingdon Press, 1938, pp. 18 ff.

70 *The King Who Polished His Crown*, op. cit., pp. 61 f.

72 *Lighthouses and Other Talks to Children*, London: Lutterworth Press, 1952, pp. 76 ff.

74 *The Fingerprints of God*, New York: Abingdon Press, 1939, pp. 121 ff.

76 *Feeling Low?*, Grand Rapids: Wm. B. Eerdmans Publishing Co., 1955, pp. 155 ff.

77 *Fifty Object Talks*, Westwood, New Jersey: Fleming H. Revell Co., 1952, pp. 36 ff.

78 *More Stories for Junior Worship*, New York: Abingdon Press, 1948, pp. 108 ff.

80 *Jack-in-the-Pulpit*, Philadelphia: The Judson Press, 1923, p. 29.

81 *Doing the Impossible*, op. cit., pp. 87 f.

82 *Stories for Junior Worship*, New York: Abingdon Press, 1941, pp. 152 ff.

83 *Good Measure*, London: James Clarke & Co. Ltd., 1945, pp. 31 ff.

84 *The Soul of a Child*, Westwood, New Jersey: Fleming H. Revell Co., 1916, pp. 21 ff.

86 *Short Sermons for Children*, New York: G. P. Putnam's Sons, 1941, pp. 5 ff.

87 *The Story Shop*, Philadelphia: The Judson Press, 1938, pp. 114 ff.

90 *Truth—to Tell*, London: Epworth Press, 1954, pp. 23 f.

91 *Forty Stories for the Church, School and Home*, New York: Harper & Brothers, 1939, pp. 96 ff.

92 *Doing the Impossible*, op. cit., pp. 69 f.

Sources

93 *The Second Book of Story Talks,* op. cit., pp. 46 ff.

94 *Fifty-two Story Sermons for Children,* New York: Harper & Brothers, 1940, pp. 27 f.

95 *Seventy-five Stories for the Worship Hour,* New York: Harper & Brothers, 1929, pp. 102 f.

97 *A Million Miles to Nowhere,* op. cit., pp. 15 ff.

98 *A Year with the Children,* op. cit., pp. 86 ff.

99 *Story Talks for Children,* Columbus: Wartburg Press, 1942, pp. 53 ff.

100 *Children's Parable Story-Sermons,* Westwood, New Jersey: Fleming H. Revell Co., 1945, pp. 105 ff.

101 *The Man at the Bell,* London: Independent Press, 1954, pp. 22 ff.

104 *Ibid.,* pp. 25 ff.

105 *The Child's World in Story-Sermons,* Westwood, New Jersey: Fleming H. Revell Co., 1938, pp. 133 ff.

106 *Tent Pegs,* New York: Abingdon Press, 1939, pp. 23 ff.

107 *More World Stories Retold,* Philadelphia: The Judson Press, 1936, pp. 195 ff.

108 *Now, Children!,* London: The Carey Kingsgate Press, Ltd., 1954, pp. 77 ff.

110 *One Year's Talks to Children,* op. cit., pp. 157 ff.

111 *When the King Came,* Boston: Houghton Mifflin Co., 1904, pp. 3 ff.

112 *Junior Sermon Stories,* op. cit., pp. 19 ff.

114 *The Use of the Story in Religious Education,* rev. ed., New York: Harper & Brothers, 1936, pp. 63 ff.

INDEX OF CONTRIBUTORS

References are to story-sermon numbers.

INDEX OF TEXTS

Scriptural references are listed by story-sermon numbers.

SPECIAL DAY INDEX

Materials appropriate for special days and occasions are listed by story-sermon numbers.

SUBJECT AND NAME INDEX

References are listed by story-sermon numbers.

Subject and Name Index

Subject and Name Index